SAMS
Teach Yourself
MICROSOFT
POWERPOINT 2000

Faithe Wempen

in 10 Minutes

SAMS

A Division of Macmillan Computer Publishing
201 West 103rd St., Indianapolis, Indiana, 46290 USA

To Margaret

SAMS TEACH YOURSELF MICROSOFT POWERPOINT 2000 IN 10 MINUTES

Copyright © 1999 by Sams Publishing

International Standard Book Number: 0-672-31440-1

Library of Congress Catalog Card Number: 98-86999

Printed in the United States of America

First Printing: May 1999

01   00   4   3   2

TRADEMARKS

EXECUTIVE EDITOR
Angela Wethington

ACQUISITIONS EDITOR
Stephanie J. McComb

DEVELOPMENT EDITOR
Valerie Perry

MANAGING EDITOR
Thomas F. Hayes

PROJECT EDITOR
Tom Stevens

COPY EDITOR
Carolyn Linn

INDEXER
Angela Williams

TECHNICAL EDITOR
Mark Hall

PROOFREADER
Debra Neel

LAYOUT TECHNICIANS
Lisa England
JoAnna LaBarge
Christy M. Lemasters

CONTENTS

INTRODUCTION

Congratulations on choosing Microsoft PowerPoint 2000! PowerPoint is one of the most powerful and flexible business-presentation programs sold today. Whether you need to create some simple text overheads for a speech at a local club or a high-impact animated show for an important business deal, PowerPoint can handle the job.

Although PowerPoint comes with many features to help the beginner, it's still not a simple program. You probably won't be able to dive right in without instructions. On the other hand, you certainly don't want to wade through a 500-page manual to find your way around.

- You want a clear-cut, plain-English introduction to PowerPoint.

- You need to create a professional-looking, usable presentation—fast.

- You don't have much time to study graphic-design theory.

You need *Sams Teach Yourself PowerPoint 2000 in 10 Minutes*.

WHAT IS MICROSOFT POWERPOINT 2000?

Microsoft PowerPoint 2000 is a graphics program designed for use with Microsoft Windows 95 or 98, Windows NT Workstation 3.51, or Windows NT 4.0. PowerPoint 2000 specializes in creating effective business presentations. Many graphics programs can help you draw, but PowerPoint can help you put text and drawings and colors and shapes together to effectively convey a message.

What Is Windows? Windows is an operating system for desktop PCs. PowerPoint 2000 runs on any version of Windows produced in the last several years, including Windows 95, Windows 98, Windows NT Workstation 3.51, or Windows NT 4.0. Other versions of PowerPoint are available for other operating systems, such as Windows 3.x (16-bit versions of the Windows operating system) and the Apple Macintosh.

The following are just a few things you can do with PowerPoint:

- Type the text for a presentation directly into PowerPoint, or import it from another program.

- Set a consistent, readable color scheme and layout for your entire presentation, or custom-design each slide.

- Create dazzling animations and transitions between slides that you can control with a few keystrokes as you give the presentation—no more fumbling with transparencies!

- Create audience handouts and speaker's notes that supplement your presentation.

- Show others your presentation onscreen, in printed form, or on the Internet.

You learn to do all of this and more in this book.

WHAT IS THE TEACH YOURSELF IN 10 MINUTES SERIES?

The *Sams Teach Yourself in 10 Minutes* series is a quick approach to learning computer programs. Instead of trying to cover the entire program, the *Sams Teach Yourself in 10 Minutes* books teach you only about the features of the program that a beginner is most likely to need.

No matter what your professional demands, *Sams Teach Yourself PowerPoint 2000 in 10 Minutes* helps you find and learn the main features of the program and become productive with it more quickly. You can learn this wonderfully logical and powerful program in a fraction of the time you would normally spend learning a new program.

INSTALLING POWERPOINT

If you received PowerPoint when you bought a new PC or when you installed Office 2000, then PowerPoint is probably already installed. Choose Start, Programs, and look for PowerPoint on the list that appears. If it's there, you're all set. If not, it's a simple matter to install PowerPoint.

Locate your PowerPoint 2000 or Office 2000 CD, and insert it in your CD-ROM drive. The installation program should start automatically. Just follow the prompts, which are very clear and self-explanatory. When prompted to restart your PC, click Yes. After Windows restarts, you're good to go.

CONVENTIONS USED IN THIS BOOK

Each of the lessons in this book includes step-by-step instructions for performing a specific task. The following icons help you identify particular types of information:

 Tips   These offer shortcuts and hints for using the program most effectively.

 Plain English   These identify new terms and definitions.

Caution These appear in places where new users often run into trouble.

Specific conventions in this book help you to easily find your way around Microsoft PowerPoint:

What you type	appears in **bold, color type**.
What you select	appears in color type.
Menu, Field, and Key names	appear with the first letter capitalized.

ACKNOWLEDGMENTS

My thanks goes out to the wonderful editors at Macmillan Computer
Publishing who tackled this project with me at such a busy time in their
schedules: Stephanie McComb, Valerie Perry, Tom Stevens, and Carolyn
Linn . Their conscientious work and attention to detail made this book a
pleasure to work on.

TELL US WHAT YOU THINK!

As the reader of this book, *you* are our most important critic and com-
mentator. We value your opinion and want to know what we're doing
right, what we could do better, what areas you'd like to see us publish
in, and any other words of wisdom you're willing to pass our way.

As the Executive Editor for the General Desktop Applications team at
Macmillan Computer Publishing, I welcome your comments. You can fax,
email, or write me directly to let me know what you did or didn't like
about this book—as well as what we can do to make our books stronger.

*Please note that I cannot help you with technical problems related to the
topic of this book, and that due to the high volume of mail I receive, I
might not be able to reply to every message.*

When you write, please be sure to include this book's title and author as
well as your name and phone or fax number. I will carefully review your
comments and share them with the author and editors who worked on the
book.

Fax: 317-581-4770

Email: office_sams@mcp.com

Mail: Executive Editor
            General Desktop Applications
            Macmillan Computer Publishing
            201 West 103rd Street
            Indianapolis, IN 46290 USA

LESSON 1

STARTING AND EXITING POWERPOINT

In this lesson, you learn how to start and exit PowerPoint.

STARTING POWERPOINT

Before you start PowerPoint, you must have PowerPoint installed on your computer, and you should have a basic understanding of the Windows 95/98 or Windows NT operating systems. This book always refers to Windows 98, but keep in mind that in most cases, if you're using Windows 95 or NT, the information applies to you too.

To start PowerPoint, follow these steps:

1. Click the Start button.

2. Move your mouse pointer to Programs. A menu of programs appears.

3. Move your mouse pointer to Microsoft PowerPoint and click it (see Figure 1.1). PowerPoint starts and displays the introductory screen shown in Figure 1.2.

The first thing you see when you start PowerPoint is a dialog box in which you choose whether you want to start a new presentation or open an existing one. You learn about this dialog box in Lesson 2, "Creating a New Presentation." For now, click Cancel to exit this dialog box.

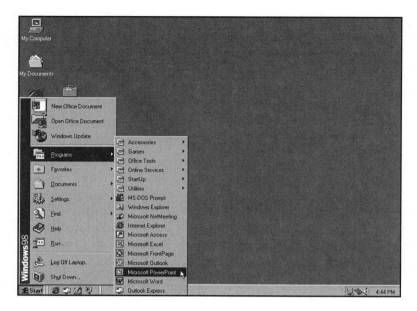

FIGURE **1.1**   To start PowerPoint, move through the Start button's menu system to Microsoft PowerPoint.

 PowerPoint Not on the Menu?   You may have speci-fied a different menu when you installed PowerPoint, or you may not have installed PowerPoint yet.

 Help! There's a Paperclip Talking to Me!   No, you haven't lost your mind. That character is one of Microsoft Office's Assistants. Occasionally the little guy gives you a suggestion, and you have to click the appropriate button below his words to move on. The first time you start PowerPoint, he might say some-thing. Press Esc to continue with your work. You learn more about the Office Assistants in Lesson 4, "Getting Help."

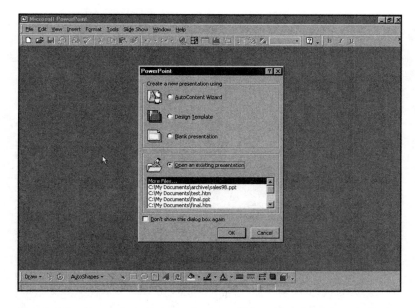

FIGURE **1.2**   PowerPoint's introductory dialog box. (You learn about it in Lesson 2.)

EXITING POWERPOINT

When you finish using PowerPoint, you should exit the program. Don't just turn off your computer, or you could create problems that could cause your PC to misbehave.

To exit PowerPoint:

1. If the PowerPoint dialog box is still onscreen, click the Cancel button to close it.

2. If this dialog box is not onscreen, do one of the following (see Figure 1.3):

   • Click the PowerPoint window's Close (X) button.

   • Double-click the Control-menu icon in the left corner of the title bar, or click it once to open the Control menu and then select Close.

- Open the File menu and select Exit.

- Press Alt+F4.

You can double-click here to close.

You can select Exit from the File menu.

You can click this Close button to close the PowerPoint window.

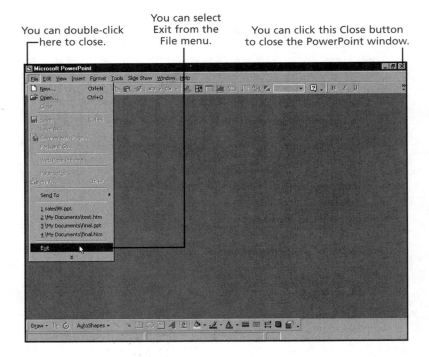

FIGURE 1.3   There are several ways to exit PowerPoint.

3. If you're asked if you want to save your changes, select Yes to save your changes. (If you choose Yes, see Lesson 6, "Saving, Closing, Opening, and Finding Presentations," to learn how to complete the Save As dialog box that appears.) Select No if you haven't created anything you want to save yet.

In this lesson, you learned to start and exit PowerPoint. In the next lesson, you learn how to create a new presentation.

LESSON 2

CREATING A NEW PRESENTATION

In this lesson, you learn how to create a presentation in several different ways.

THREE CHOICES FOR STARTING A NEW PRESENTATION

PowerPoint offers several ways to create a new presentation. Before you begin, decide on the method that's right for you:

- **AutoContent Wizard** offers the highest degree of help. It walks you through each step of creating the new presentation. When you're finished you have a standardized group of slides, all with a similar look and feel, for a particular situation. Each template slide includes dummy text that you can replace with your own text.

- A design template provides a professionally designed color, background, and font scheme, which apply to the slides you create yourself. It does not provide sample slides.

- You can choose to start from scratch and create a totally blank presentation, but building a presentation from the ground up is not recommended for beginners.

Wizards   Wizards are a special feature that most Microsoft products offer. A wizard displays a series of dialog boxes that ask you design and content questions. You select options and type text. When you are done, the wizard creates something (in this case, a presentation) according to your instructions.

Design Template   A design template is a preformatted presentation file (without any slides in it). When you select a template, PowerPoint applies the color scheme and general layout of the template to each slide in the presentation.

A WORD ABOUT THE POWERPOINT DIALOG BOX

If you have just started PowerPoint and the PowerPoint dialog box is displayed, you are ready to start a new presentation (see Figure 2.1). From here, you can choose to create a new presentation using the AutoContent Wizard, a Design Template, or a Blank presentation. Just click your choice, click OK, and follow along with the steps in the remainder of this lesson to complete the presentation.

Unfortunately, this dialog box is available only when you first start the program. Once you close the dialog box, you won't see it again until the next time you start the program. That's why the steps in the remainder of this lesson don't rely on it; instead, they show alternative methods for starting a presentation if this dialog box is not available.

FIGURE 2.1   When you first start PowerPoint, this dialog box greets you. It's one method you can use to create a new presentation.

CREATING A NEW PRESENTATION WITH THE AUTOCONTENT WIZARD

With the AutoContent Wizard, you select the type of presentation you want to create (such as strategy, sales, training, conveying bad news, or general) and PowerPoint creates an outline for the presentation.

Quick Start   You can click the AutoContent Wizard button in the PowerPoint dialog box shown in Figure 2.1, click OK, and then skip the first three steps in the following procedure.

Here's how you use the AutoContent Wizard:

1. Open the File menu and click New. The New Presentation dialog box appears.

2. Click the General tab if it's not already on top. (See Figure 2.2.)

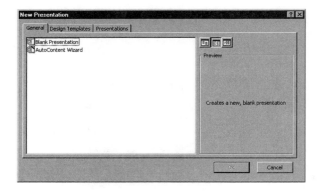

FIGURE 2.2   You can start a new presentation from here.

3. Double-click the AutoContent Wizard icon. The AutoContent Wizard starts.

Macro Warning   At step 3, you may get a warning message about macros possibly carrying viruses. Just click Enable Macros to continue.

4. Click the Next button to begin.

5. In the dialog box that appears (see Figure 2.3), click the button that best represents the type of presentation you want to create (for example, Sales/Marketing).

6. Click a presentation on the list that further narrows your presentation's purpose (for example, Marketing Plan). Then click Next.

7. Choose the method that best describes how you will give the presentation:

   • Onscreen presentation   Choose this if you plan to use a computer and your PowerPoint file to present the show.

   • Web presentation   Choose this if you are planning to distribute the presentation as a self-running or user-interactive show.

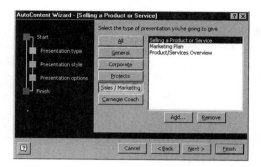

FIGURE 2.3   Just answer the AutoContent Wizard's questions and click Next.

- Black and white overheads   Choose this if you plan to make black-and-white transparencies for your show.

- Color overheads   Choose this if you plan to make color transparencies for your show.

- 35mm slides   Choose this if you plan to send your PowerPoint presentation to a service bureau to have 35mm slides made. (You probably don't have such expensive and specialized equipment in your own company.)

8. Click Next to continue.

9. Enter the presentation title in the field provided.

10. (Optional) If you want to include a footer (repeated text) on each slide, enter the text in the Footer text box.

11. (Optional) If you do not want a date or slide number on each slide, deselect the Date last updated or Slide number check boxes.

12. Click Finish. The beginnings of your presentation, with dummy text in place, appear onscreen in Normal view. (You learn about Normal view, as well as other views, in Lesson 5, "Working with Slides in Different Views.")

Replacing Dummy Text   You can start personalizing your presentation right away by replacing the dummy text with your own text. Just select the existing text and type right over it. See Lesson 11, "Adding Text to a Slide," for more information about editing text.

CREATING A NEW PRESENTATION WITH A DESIGN TEMPLATE

A template is the middle ground between maximum hand-holding (the AutoContent Wizard) and no help at all (Blank Presentation).

There are two kinds of templates: presentation templates and design templates. When you use the AutoContent Wizard, you use a presentation template. It contains not only formatting, but also sample slides. The other kind of template is a design template. It contains formatting only—no slides. If you want to use a presentation template, use the AutoContent Wizard, as explained in the preceding section.

To start a new presentation using a design template, follow these steps:

1. Open the File menu and select New. The New dialog box opens.

2. Click the Design Templates tab. A list of design templates appears.

3. Click a template. A preview of the template appears in the Preview area. Click each of the templates in turn, to locate one you like.

Installing Templates On-the-Fly   If you get a message that the template you have chosen is not installed, prompting you to install it, click Yes and let the Office 2000 installation program set up the template for you. You must have the Office 2000 CD in your drive to do this.

4. After you select the template you want to use, click OK. PowerPoint creates the new presentation based on that template.

5. The New Slide dialog box appears, prompting you for the layout of the first slide (see Figure 2.4). Select the AutoLayout you want to use, and click OK.

Choose this one to make up your own layout.

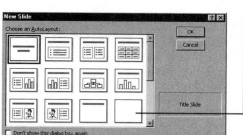

FIGURE 2.4   In the New Slide dialog box, you can choose a pre-designed slide layout, or you can choose to design your own.

 The Next Step?   Add more slides by clicking the New Slide button on the toolbar, creating your presentation one slide at a time. (See Lesson 10, "Inserting, Deleting, and Copying Slides," for help).

CREATING A BLANK PRESENTATION

Are you sure you want to attempt a blank presentation on your first time out? A blank presentation has no preset color scheme or design, and no dummy text to help you decide what to write. To create a blank presentation, follow these steps:

1. Open the File menu and select New.

2. Click the General tab.

3. Double-click the Blank Presentation icon. The New Slide dialog box appears (refer to Figure 2.4).

4. Select the AutoLayout you want to use, click it, and click OK.

WHAT'S NEXT?

Now you have the basic shell of your presentation, but you need to modify and customize it. If you're not in a hurry, read the lessons in this book to learn PowerPoint fully. However, if you're in a hurry, refer to the following lessons:

- To change the view of the presentation so that you can work with it more easily, see Lesson 5, "Working with Slides in Different Views."

- To apply a different design template or slide layout, see Lesson 8, "Changing a Presentation's Look."

- To add new slides, see Lesson 10, "Inserting, Deleting, and Copying Slides."

- To add and edit text, see Lesson 11, "Adding Text to a Slide."

In this lesson, you learned how to create a new presentation. In the next lesson, you learn how to control the PowerPoint program with menus and toolbars.

LESSON 3

GETTING AROUND IN POWERPOINT

In this lesson, you learn about the PowerPoint application and presentation windows and how to enter commands with shortcut menus and toolbars.

A LOOK AT POWERPOINT'S APPLICATION WINDOW

Now that you have some sort of presentation started, let's take a look at the PowerPoint window. Your presentation appears in the center, of course, and all around it are tools that help you issue commands and perform modifications to it.

Some of the controls are standard Windows ones, such as the title bar, the window control buttons (Minimize, Maximize, and Close), and the menu system. In addition, you see some toolbars and several other items that are unique to PowerPoint. You learn about these screen elements in this lesson and in upcoming ones.

WORKING WITH MENUS

You are probably already familiar with menus. To open a menu, click its name on the menu bar, and then click the command you want to issue.

However, in Office 2000 programs like PowerPoint, the menus have a special feature. When you open a menu, the entire menu does not display right away; only a select list of commands appears. If you pause a moment, or click the down-pointing arrow at the bottom of the menu, the entire menu unfurls, showing the remaining commands. This is called an *adaptive* menu because it adapts to the way you use the program. For example, in Figure 3.1, the menu on the left is the one that opens initially, and the one on the right is the full version that opens a few seconds later.

Figure 3.1   The most common or recently used commands appear first (left), and then the full menu a few seconds later (right).

Which Comes First?   A core set of essential commands always appears on the initial menu. In addition, any command that you have recently used also appears first. That way, over time, PowerPoint "learns" which commands you use most often, and displays them first.

Because a menu's commands vary depending on what actions you have taken, the figures in this book show the menus with the personalized feature turned off. To turn this feature off yourself, open the Tools menu and choose Customize. Then on the Options tab, deselect the Menus show recently used commands first check box. (This is the same dialog box you use later in this lesson, in the section "Separating the Standard and Formatting Toolbars.")

WORKING WITH TOOLBARS

A *toolbar* is a collection of buttons that enables you to bypass the menu system. For example, instead of selecting File, Save (opening the File menu and selecting Save), you can click the Save toolbar button to save your work. You learn more about toolbars later in this lesson.

PowerPoint displays three toolbars in Normal view: the Standard and Formatting toolbars below the menu bar and the Drawing toolbar at the bottom of the screen. In other views, or while certain features are active, you may see additional toolbars.

To select a button from the toolbar, just click the button.

By default in PowerPoint 2000, the Standard and Formatting toolbars appear on the same line, and most of the buttons on the Standard toolbar are not visible. To view the undisplayed buttons, you must click the >> button at the right end of that toolbar to open a pop-up list of them, as shown in Figure 3.2.

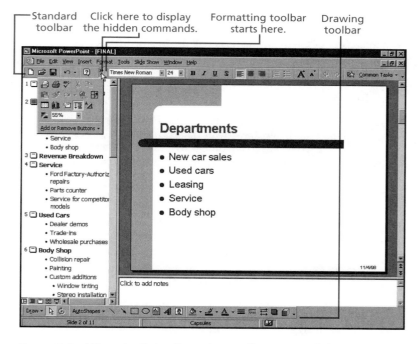

FIGURE 3.2   When both toolbars share a line, most of the tools on the Standard toolbar are hidden until you pop them up.

SEPARATING THE STANDARD AND FORMATTING TOOLBARS

Many people prefer to have each toolbar on a separate line, as was the default in earlier versions of PowerPoint. To do so, follow these steps:

1. Open the Tools menu and choose Customize. The Customize dialog box appears.

2. Click the Options tab.

3. Click to remove the check mark in the Standard and Formatting toolbars share one row check box.

4. Click Close. The toolbars appear on separate rows.

The remainder of the figures in this book use this two-row toolbar configuration because you can see the tools being referenced more easily.

LEARNING MORE ABOUT A TOOLBAR BUTTON

To see the name of a button, move the mouse pointer over the button. PowerPoint displays a ScreenTip that provides the name of the button.

To learn more about a button, press Shift+F1 or select Help, What's This? and then click the button for which you want more information.

TURNING TOOLBARS ON OR OFF

If you never use a particular toolbar, you can turn it off to free up some screen space. In addition, you can turn on other toolbars that come with PowerPoint but don't appear automatically. To turn a toolbar on or off, do the following:

1. Right-click any toolbar. A shortcut menu appears (see Figure 3.3). A check mark appears beside each toolbar that is turned on.

2. Click the displayed toolbar you want to hide, or click a hidden toolbar that you want to display. Check marks appear beside displayed toolbars.

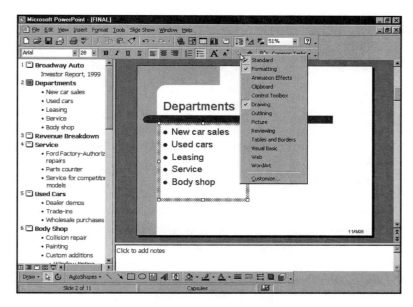

3.3   The shortcut menu for toolbars displays the names of all the toolbars.

When you click a toolbar name on the menu, the menu disappears and that toolbar appears (if it was hidden) or the toolbar disappears (if it was displayed).

USING SHORTCUT MENUS

Although you can enter all commands in PowerPoint using menus, PowerPoint offers a quicker way: context-sensitive shortcut menus like the ones in Windows. To use a shortcut menu, move the mouse pointer over the object you want the command to act on, and then click the right mouse button. A shortcut menu pops up, just as it did for the toolbars in Figure 3.3, offering commands that pertain to the selected object. Click the desired command. For example, Figure 3.4 shows the menu you get when you right-click some text on a slide.

I right-clicked this text.

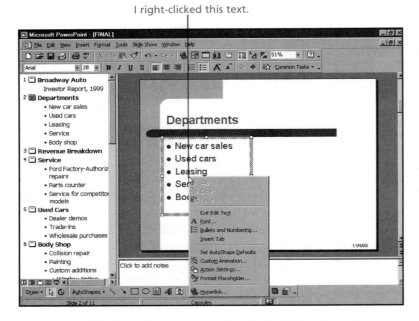

FIGURE 3.4   Display a shortcut menu by right-clicking the object.

WORKING WITH THE PRESENTATION WINDOW

In the center of the PowerPoint window is your presentation. Its window contains one or more panes, depending on the view in use. Figure 3.5 shows Normal view, which contains three panes: Outline, Slide, and Notes. You learn more about this and other views in Lesson 5, "Working with Slides in Different Views."

 Turning Off the Office Assistant   The Office Assistant (by default it's Clippit, the paperclip) provides help as you work. If you don't want the Office Assistant onscreen all the time, you can easily make it disappear. Right-click it and choose Hide. To make it reappear, select Help, Show the Office Assistant. You learn more about the Office Assistant in Lesson 4, "Getting Help."

Outline
pane   Notes pane   Slide pane   Office Assistant

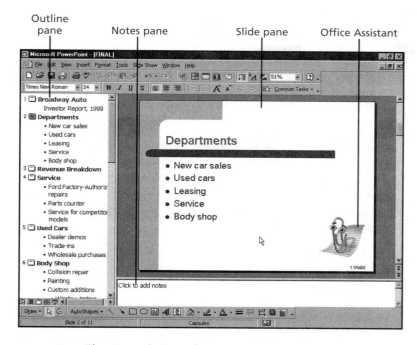

FIGURE 3.5   The Normal view of the presentation shows the Outline, Slide, and Notes panes.

As you learn in Lesson 5, you can edit the presentation's text either in the Outline or the Slide pane. Changes in one pane affect the other. If you want to place a non-text object on a slide (such as a graphic), you do so in the Slide pane. The Notes pane provides a space for entering your own notes, which will not be visible to your audience.

In this lesson, you learned about the PowerPoint application and presentation windows, and you learned how to enter commands with shortcut menus and toolbars. In the next lesson, you learn how to use the PowerPoint Help system.

LESSON 4
GETTING HELP

In this lesson, you learn about the various types of help available to you in PowerPoint.

HELP: WHAT'S AVAILABLE?

Because every person is different, PowerPoint offers many ways to get help with the program. You can use any of these methods to get help:

- Ask the Office Assistant for help.

- Choose what you're interested in learning about from a series of Help topics.

- Get help on a particular element you see onscreen with the What's This? tool.

USING THE OFFICE ASSISTANT

You probably have already met the Office Assistant; it's Clippit, the paperclip that pops up to give you advice. Don't let its whimsical appearance fool you, though; behind the Office Assistant is a very powerful Help system.

DISPLAYING OR HIDING THE OFFICE ASSISTANT

By default, the Office Assistant is turned on and sits on top of whatever you're working on. You can turn it off by right-clicking it and choosing Hide (see Figure 4.1). To redisplay the Office Assistant, choose Help, Show the Office Assistant. If the Office Assistant is ever in your way but you don't want to hide it, drag it with your mouse to a different spot onscreen.

Office Assistant

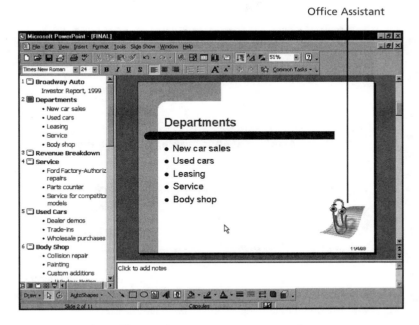

FIGURE 4.1 The Office Assistant appears on top of your presentation window.

 More Assistants Available To change the Office Assistant character, right-click the current assistant and select Choose Assistant (if you don't like paper-clips, for instance).

THE KINDS OF HELP OFFICE ASSISTANT PROVIDES

When you click the Office Assistant, a bubble appears next to (or above) its box asking you what kind of help you want (see Figure 4.2). You can do any of the following:

- Type a question or keyword in the text box to tell the Office Assistant what kind of help you need. (More on this shortly.)

FIGURE 4.2   Office Assistant at your service, asking what you need help with.

- Click the Options button to customize the way the Office Assistant works. (More about this later in this lesson.)

- Click away from the bubble to close the bubble but leave the Office Assistant onscreen.

 If you close the help bubble, you can reopen it at any time by clicking the Help button on the Standard toolbar, pressing F1, selecting Help, Microsoft PowerPoint Help, or clicking the Office Assistant.

 Extra Tips Along the Way   Sometimes you'll see a light bulb over the Office Assistant's head. This means that the Office Assistant has a suggestion for you regarding the task that you're currently performing. To get the suggestion, just click the light bulb.

ASKING THE OFFICE ASSISTANT A QUESTION

If you need help on a particular topic, simply type a question into the text box shown in Figure 4.2. Follow these steps:

1. If the Office Assistant's help bubble doesn't appear, click the Office Assistant or press F1.

2. Type a question into the text box. For instance, you might type **How do I save?** to get help saving your work.

3. Press Enter or click the Search button. The Office Assistant provides some topics that might match what you're looking for. For example, Figure 4.3 shows the Office Assistant's answer to the question "How do I save?".

What would you like to do?
- About where to save on the Web
- Troubleshoot saving a presentation
- Save a presentation to an FTP site
- About saving presentations
- Save a presentation
▼ See more...

How do I save?

| Options | Search |

FIGURE 4.3   The Office Assistant asks you to narrow exactly what you are trying to accomplish, so it can provide the best help possible.

4. Click the option that best describes what you're trying to do. For example, I'm going to choose Save a presentation from Figure 4.3. A Help window appears with instructions for the specified task.

If none of the options describe what you want, click the See more arrow to view more options, or type in a different question in the text box.

5. If another list of topics appears, click a link to further narrow down the help you want.

6. Read the instructions that appear. Then close the Microsoft PowerPoint Help window (click the X button at the upper-right corner of the screen) or click the Office Assistant again and search for something else.

For more information about working with the Microsoft PowerPoint Help window, see "Using the Microsoft PowerPoint Help Window" later in this chapter.

TURNING OFF THE OFFICE ASSISTANT FEATURE

By default, whenever you access the Help system in PowerPoint, you do so using the Office Assistant. However, some people just can't stand dealing with a cartoon character, or are more advanced users who want more power and flexibility in using the Help system. If that's you, turn the Office Assistant off altogether:

1. Right-click the Office Assistant and choose Options.

2. In the Office Assistant dialog box that appears, deselect the Use the Office Assistant check box.

3. Click OK.

When you turn off the Office Assistant, all the normal ways of activating the assistant (F1, the Help, Microsoft PowerPoint Help command, and so on) activate the Microsoft PowerPoint Help window instead.

USING THE MICROSOFT POWERPOINT HELP WINDOW

After the Microsoft PowerPoint Help window is open (from one of the Office Assistant's searches), you can browse the Help system on your own. If you have used an earlier version of a Microsoft Office product, you may be familiar with the Contents, Index, and Find mechanisms that used to be the hallmark of a Microsoft product's Help system. These are still available in Office 2000 programs like PowerPoint, but in a slightly different form.

If you are using an Office Assistant, the only way to get into the main Help system is by asking a question, as you learned to do earlier in this lesson. However, if you turn off the Office Assistant, as explained in the preceding section, then choosing Help, Microsoft PowerPoint Help will access the Help system directly.

If you are using the Help system from an Office Assistant query, click the Show/Hide button in the Help window's toolbar, pointed out in Figure 4.4, to expand the Help controls you need in the following sections.

THE CONTENTS TAB

The Contents tab of the Help system is a series of "books" you can open. Each book has one or more Help topics in it. Figure 4.4 shows the Contents tab.

Click a plus sign to open a book.
Show/Hide button   The help articles appear here to be read.

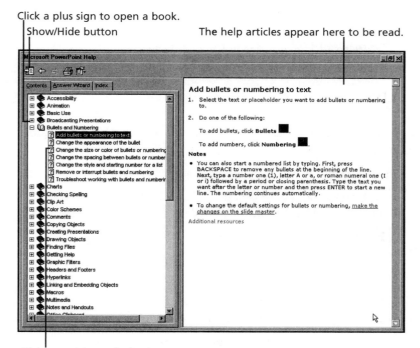

Click an article to display it.

FIGURE 4.4   The Help Contents panel is a group of books that contain Help information.

To select a Help topic from the Contents screen, follow these steps:

1. If you do not see the Contents, Answer Wizard, and Index tabs shown in Figure 4.4, click the Show button on the Help window's toolbar.

2. Click the Contents tab.

3. Find the book that describes, in broad terms, what you're looking for help with.

4. Double-click the book. A list of Help articles appears below the book, as shown in Figure 4.4.

5. Click a Help article to display it.

6. After reading that article, display and read another, or close the Help system by clicking its Close (X) button.

THE ANSWER WIZARD TAB

The Answer Wizard is just like the Office Assistant, except without the cartoon character. You can ask it a question in ordinary language, just like you can the Office Assistant.

To use the Answer Wizard, follow these steps:

1. If you do not see the tabbed sections in the Help window, click the Show button on the Help window's toolbar.

2. Click the Answer Wizard tab.

3. Type your question in the What would you like to do? box, and click Search.

4. Browse through the topics that appear in the bottom box, and click the one that matches the help you need (see Figure 4.5).

5. After reading the article, display and read another, or close the Help system by clicking its Close (X) button.

THE INDEX TAB

The Index is an alphabetical listing of every Help topic available. It's like an index in a book. To use the Index, follow these steps:

1. If you do not see the tabbed sections in the Help window, click the Show button on the Help window's toolbar.

2. Click the Index tab.

Type a word here.
The list jumps to match (as closely as possible) what you typed.

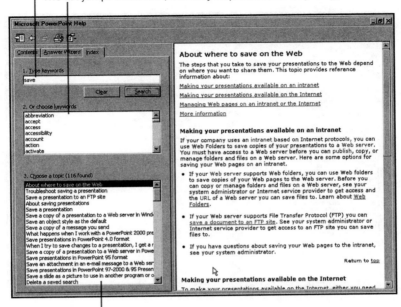

Topics found appear here.

FIGURE 4.5   Browse through topics alphabetically with the Index.

3. Type the first few letters of the topic you want to find. The index list jumps quickly to that spot.

4. Click the Search button. A list of topics (articles) that include the chosen keyword appears (see Figure 4.5).

5. Click a topic to display it.

6. After reading an article, display and read another, or close the Help system by clicking its Close (X) button.

Back button   Options button
  Print button   Type your question.

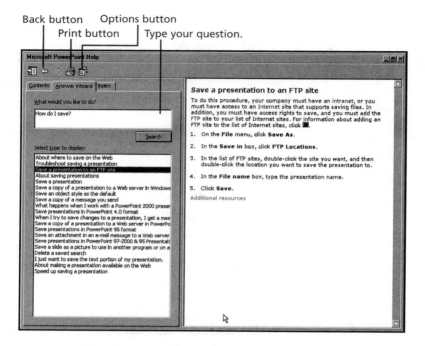

FIGURE 4.6   Use the Answer Wizard to locate all the Help topics that deal with a certain subject.

READING A HELP TOPIC

No matter which of the avenues you choose for finding a help topic (the Office Assistant, Contents, Answer Wizard, or Index), you eventually end up at an article you can read, like the one in the right pane of Figure 4.6. From here, you can read the information onscreen or do any of the following:

- Click a colored word to see a definition of it. For example, in Figure 4.6, the colored words are **intranet, Internet,** and **FTP**.

- Click a >> button to jump to another Help screen. For example, in Figure 4.6, there is a >> button at the end of the first paragraph.

- Click an underlined word or phrase to jump to another Help screen. This works the same as a >> button; it is simply an alternative that some Help topics use.

- Click a Show Me link to make the Help system perform the step for you.

- Print a hard copy of the information by clicking the Print button on the Help window's toolbar (the button that looks like a printer).

- Copy the text to the Clipboard (for pasting into a program such as Microsoft Word or Windows Notepad) by clicking the Options button (the rightmost button) and then selecting Copy.

- Return to the previous Help topic you viewed by clicking the Back button (the left-pointing arrow button). If you have not looked at other Help topics this session, the Back button is not available.

- Close the Help window by clicking the Close (X) button.

FINDING AND FIXING ERRORS IN THE PROGRAM

A new feature in Office 2000 is Detect and Repair. It can identify problems with your copy of PowerPoint, such as a damaged program file or corrupted driver, and repair the problem using your original Office 2000 or PowerPoint 2000 disk. This repair process can take a long time (30 minutes or more), so don't perform it unless you suspect problems.

If PowerPoint starts behaving strangely, the best thing to do is close PowerPoint and restart Windows. If you are still having trouble, follow these steps:

1. Choose Help, Detect and Repair.

2. An explanation box appears. Click Start.

3. Wait for the utility to compare all your PowerPoint files to the original ones on the CD and to check for errors. Be patient; this takes a long time.

4. When you see a message that you must restart the system for the changes to take effect, click Yes.

OTHER HELP FEATURES

Let's finish up this lesson by looking at a few of the Help features that you may not use as frequently but are still very useful.

GETTING HELP WITH SCREEN ELEMENTS

If you wonder what a particular button or tool on the screen is used for, wonder no more. Just follow these steps:

1. Select Help, What's This? or press Shift+F1.

2. Click the screen element for which you want help. A box appears explaining the element.

GETTING MORE HELP ON THE WEB

Whenever you use the Office Assistant, one of the choices on the second "page" of search results (which you display by clicking See more) is None of the above, look for more help on the Web. If you choose that, and you have an Internet connection, Internet Explorer opens and jumps to the Microsoft Web site, where you can look up more information.

You can also go to the Microsoft Web site without having a particular question in mind by selecting Help, Microsoft on the Web.

In this lesson, you learned about the many ways that PowerPoint offers help. In the next lesson, you learn about the different views PowerPoint offers for working with your presentation.

LESSON 5

WORKING WITH SLIDES IN DIFFERENT VIEWS

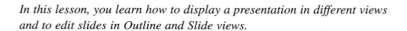

In this lesson, you learn how to display a presentation in different views and to edit slides in Outline and Slide views.

CHANGING VIEWS

PowerPoint can display your presentation in different views. Having the option of selecting a view makes it easier to perform certain tasks. For example, Normal view has Outline, Slide, and Notes panes, suitable for working on the text of each slide and for placing objects on a slide, whereas Slide Sorter view enables you to quickly rearrange the slides. Figure 5.1 shows some of the different views.

To change views, open the View menu and choose the desired view: Normal, Slide Sorter, Notes Page, or Slide Show.

> **Normal**   The default, 3-pane view. Variations of it include Outline view and Slide view.
>
> **Slide Sorter**   Shows all the slides as thumbnail sketches, so you can easily rearrange them.
>
> **Notes Page**   Provides a large pane for creating notes for your speech. You can also type these notes in Normal view, but Notes Page view gives you more room.
>
> **Slide Show**   A specialized view that enables you to preview and present your show onscreen. You won't have much use for it until later, when your show is complete.

Normal   Notes Page   Slide Show   Slide Sorter

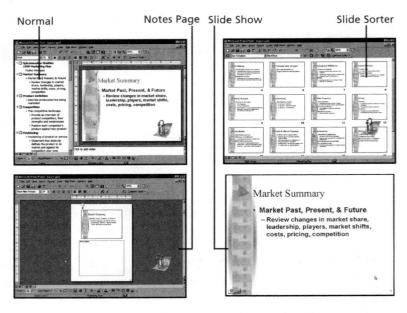

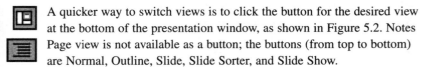

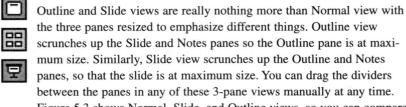

FIGURE 5.1   You can change views to make a task easier.

A quicker way to switch views is to click the button for the desired view at the bottom of the presentation window, as shown in Figure 5.2. Notes Page view is not available as a button; the buttons (from top to bottom) are Normal, Outline, Slide, Slide Sorter, and Slide Show.

Outline and Slide views are really nothing more than Normal view with the three panes resized to emphasize different things. Outline view scrunches up the Slide and Notes panes so the Outline pane is at maximum size. Similarly, Slide view scrunches up the Outline and Notes panes, so that the slide is at maximum size. You can drag the dividers between the panes in any of these 3-pane views manually at any time. Figure 5.3 shows Normal, Slide, and Outline views, so you can compare them.

No Notes?   Notice that in Slide view, the Notes pane has been effectively "resized" out of existence, but the divider line is still at the bottom of the Slide pane, and you can drag the divider up to reopen the Notes pane.

View buttons   Drag the dividers between panes in any multipane view.

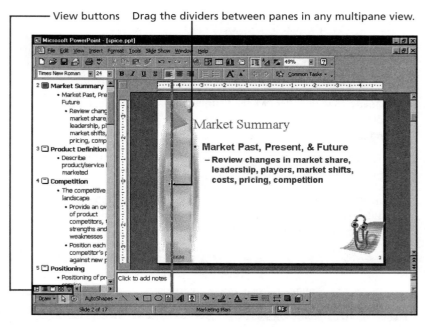

FIGURE 5.2   Use these buttons to change views.

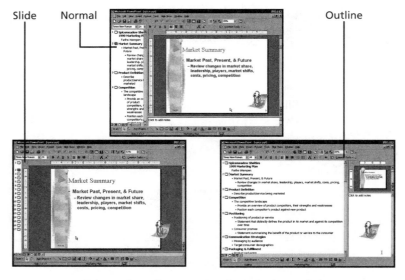

FIGURE 5.3   Slide and Outline are simply variations of the 3-pane Normal view.

MOVING FROM SLIDE TO SLIDE

When you have more than one slide in your presentation, you need to move from one slide to the next to work with a specific slide. The procedure for selecting a slide is determined by the view you are using:

- In any view that displays the Outline pane, scroll through the outline and click the text for the slide you want to see. The other panes will jump to display it.

- In any view except Slide Sorter, press Page Up or Page Down to move to the previous or next slide.

- In any view except Slide Sorter and Slide Show, click the Previous Slide or Next Slide button, just below the vertical scrollbar (as shown in Figure 5.4), or drag the box inside the scrollbar until the desired slide number is displayed.

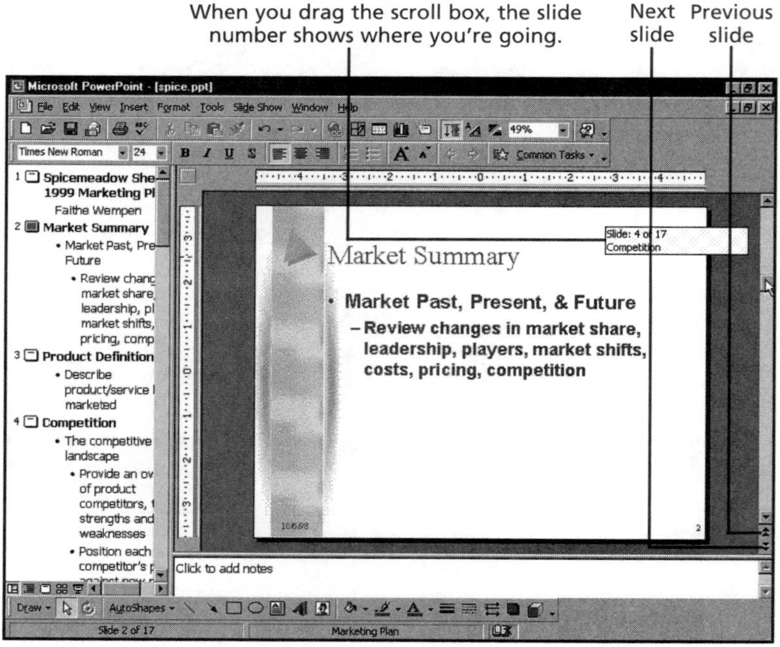

FIGURE 5.4   Use the Previous Slide and Next Slide buttons to move between slides, or drag the scroll box.

- In Slide Sorter view, click the desired slide. A thick border appears around the selected slide.

Editing Slides

If you created a presentation in Lesson 2 using the AutoContent Wizard, you already have several slides, but they may not contain the text you want to use. If you created a blank presentation or based a new presentation on a design template, you have at least one slide on the screen that you can edit.

The following sections explain how to edit text. In later lessons, you learn how to add and edit text objects, pictures, graphs, organizational charts, and other items.

 Object   An object is any item on a slide, including text, graphics, and charts.

Editing Text in the Outline Pane

The Outline pane provides the easiest way to edit text. You simply click to move the insertion point where you want it in the outline, and then type in your text. Press the Del key to delete characters to the right of the insertion point or the Backspace key to delete characters to the left.

 Larger Outline   You may want to enlarge the Outline pane by dragging its divider to the right or by clicking the Outline View button. Outline view is in use in Figure 5.5.

 Auto Word Select   When you select text, PowerPoint selects whole words. If you want to select individual characters, open the Tools menu, select Options, click the Edit tab, and click the When selecting, automatically select entire word check box to turn it off. Click OK.

Selected text

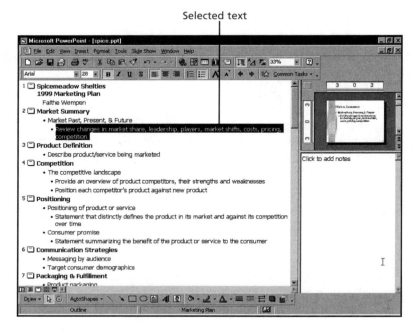

FIGURE 5.5   You can edit your text on the Outline.

MOVING A LINE IN OUTLINE VIEW

As you work in Outline view, you may find that some slides need to be rearranged. One easy way is to drag a slide by its slide icon (next to its title on the Outline) to a new position.

You can also turn on the Outlining toolbar and use its Move Up and Move Down buttons. To turn on the toolbar, right-click one of the other toolbars and choose Outlining. Then use these buttons, as shown in Figure 5.6:

- To move a paragraph up in the outline, select it, then click the Move Up button.

- To move a paragraph down in the outline, select it, and click the Move Down button.

Promote   Demote   Move Up   Move Down

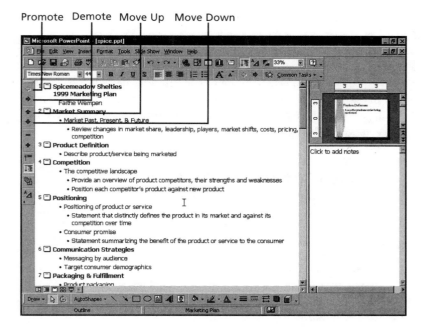

FIGURE 5.6   You can display an Outlining toolbar and use its buttons to alter the outline.

CHANGING THE TEXT'S OUTLINE LEVEL

As you can see from Figure 5.6, your presentation is organized in a multilevel outline format. The slides are at the top level of the outline, and each slide's contents are subordinate under that slide. Some slides have multiple levels of subordination (for example, a bulleted list within a bulleted list).

You can easily change an object's level in Outline view with the Tab key or the Outlining toolbar:

- **To demote a paragraph in the outline**   Click the text, then press the Tab key or click the Demote button on the Outlining toolbar.

- **To promote a paragraph in the outline**   Click the text, and then press Shift+Tab or click the Promote button on the Outlining toolbar.

In most cases, subordinate items on a slide appear as items in a bulleted list. In Lesson 12, "Creating Columns and Lists," you learn how to change the appearance of the bullet and the size and formatting of text for each entry, as well as how much the text is indented for each level.

> **Dragging Paragraphs**   You can quickly change the level of a paragraph by dragging it left or right.

EDITING TEXT IN THE SLIDE PANE

Text appears on a slide in a text box. (All objects appear on a slide in their own boxes, for easy manipulation.) As shown in Figure 5.7, to edit text on a slide, click the text box to select it, and then click where you want the insertion point moved.

When you work with the Slide pane, you may want to use Slide view or manually adjust the pane sizes. Figure 5.7 shows Slide view in use.

In Lesson 11, "Adding Text to a Slide," you learn more about adding text to a slide, including creating your own text boxes on a slide. Then in Lessons 12, "Creating Columns and Lists," and 13, "Changing the Look of Your Text," you learn how to fine-tune the look of your text for maximum impact.

You can also edit graphics on a slide in the Slide pane. Editing graphics is trickier than editing text. Lesson 16, "Adding Clip Art and Other Images," discusses placing graphics on slides, and Lessons 19, "Positioning and Sizing Objects," and 20, "Formatting Objects," cover manipulating graphics.

In this lesson, you learned how to change views for a presentation, move from slide to slide, and edit text. In the next lesson, you learn how to save, close, and open a presentation.

Text box

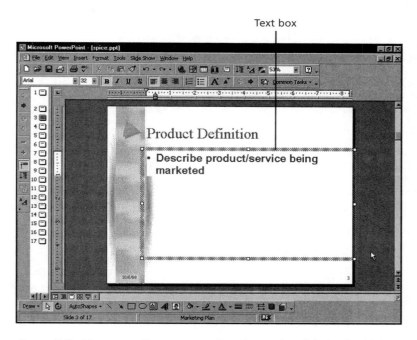

FIGURE **5.7**   You can edit your text directly on the slide in the Slide pane.

LESSON 6

SAVING, CLOSING, OPENING, AND FINDING PRESENTATIONS

In this lesson, you learn how to save a presentation to disk, close a presentation, and open an existing presentation.

SAVING A PRESENTATION

Soon after creating a presentation, you should save it on disk to protect the work you have already done. To save a presentation for the first time, follow these steps:

1. Select File, Save, or press Ctrl+S, or click the Save button on the Standard toolbar. The Save As dialog box appears.

2. In the File name text box, type the name you want to assign to the presentation. Do not type a file extension; PowerPoint automatically adds the extension .ppt (see Figure 6.1).

Long File Names   Because PowerPoint 2000 is a 32-bit application, you are not limited to the old 8-character file names, as you were with PowerPoint versions designed for Windows 3.x. Your file names can be as long as you like (within reason—the limit is 255 characters) and can include spaces.

Type the file name here.

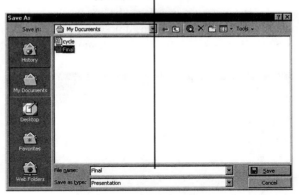

FIGURE 6.1   The Save As dialog box.

3. The Save In box shows which folder the file will be saved in. The default is My Documents. If you want to save to a different drive or folder, see the next section in this lesson. Otherwise, continue to step 4.

4. Click Save.

Now that you have named the file and saved it to a disk, you can save any changes you make simply by pressing Ctrl+S or clicking the Save button on the Standard toolbar. Your data is saved under the file name you assigned.

To create a copy of a presentation under a different name, select File, Save As. The Save As dialog box reappears, and you can use it in the same way you did when you originally saved the file.

CHANGING THE DRIVE OR FOLDER

The dialog boxes for opening and saving files in Office 2000 programs are different from the ones in Windows 95/98 in general. The Save As and Open dialog boxes take a bit of getting used to.

To change to a different drive, you must open the Save In or Look In drop-down list. (The name changes depending on whether you're saving or opening a file.) Figure 6.2 shows this drop-down list in the Save As dialog box. From it, choose the drive on which you want to save the file.

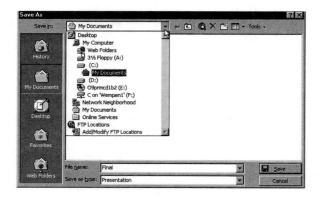

FIGURE 6.2   Use this drop-down list to choose a different drive.

Next, you must select the folder where you want to save the file (or open it from). When you select the drive, a list of the folders on that drive appears. Double-click the folder you want to select.

Table 6.1 explains the buttons and other controls you see in the Save As and Open dialog boxes.

TABLE 6.1   BUTTONS FOR CHANGING DRIVES AND FOLDERS IN
WINDOWS 95 DIALOG BOXES

CONTROL	NAME	PURPOSE
⬅	Back	Moves back to the preceding folder you looked at, if there is one. Otherwise, this button is unavailable.
⬆	Up One Level	Moves to the folder "above" the one shown in the Save In box (that is, the folder in which the current one resides).

CONTROL	NAME	PURPOSE
	Search the Web	Opens Internet Explorer, so you can search the Web for a file; seldom used.
	Delete	Deletes the selected file.
	Create New Folder	Creates a new folder.
	Views	Opens a list of viewing options for the file list (List, Details, Properties, and Preview).
Tools	Tools	Opens a menu of commands you can issue for the selected file (Delete, Rename, Print, and others).

In addition to the buttons across the top of the Save As and Open dialog boxes, there are also shortcut icons along the left side. These point to folders that some people use to store files or shortcuts to files:

- **History** Contains shortcuts for all the files you have used recently. This corresponds roughly to the Recently Used Documents list on the Start menu in Windows.

- **My Documents** The default folder for storing PowerPoint presentations. Use this button to jump back there from some other folder you may have been browsing.

- **Desktop** The folder that contains all the shortcuts on your Windows desktop. (You would seldom store a file there.)

- **Favorites** A folder that contains shortcuts to all the files you have indicated you wanted there. You can add a shortcut to the Favorites folder by opening the Tools menu in the Save As or Open dialog box and choosing Add to Favorites.

- **Web Folders** A special-purpose folder that holds any shortcuts to Web locations where you store files.

CLOSING A PRESENTATION

You can close a presentation at any time. If you are working on multiple presentations, it's okay to keep them all open at once. The more presentations you have open, however, the slower PowerPoint's response time to your commands will be, so you should close any presentations that you are not working on.

Note that although this closes the presentation window, it does not exit PowerPoint. To close a presentation, follow these steps:

1. If more than one presentation is open, open the Window menu and select the one you want to close.

2. Choose File, Close, press Ctrl+F4, or click the presentation's Close (X) button. (If you see two X buttons, it's the lower of the two.) If you have not saved the presentation, or if you haven't saved since you made changes, a dialog box appears asking if you want to save.

3. To save your changes, click Yes. If this is a new presentation, refer to the steps earlier in this lesson for saving a presentation. If you have saved the file previously, the presentation window closes.

OPENING A PRESENTATION

After you save a presentation to a disk, you can open the presentation and continue working on it at any time. Follow these steps:

1. Choose File, Open, or press Ctrl+O, or click the Open button on the Standard toolbar. The Open dialog box appears (see Figure 6.3).

2. If the file isn't in the currently displayed folder, change drives or folders. Refer to "Changing the Drive or Folder," earlier in this lesson.

3. Double-click the file to open it.

FIGURE 6.3   Select the presentation you want to open.

You can open files from some other presentation programs in PowerPoint, such as Freelance.

 New Feature In PowerPoint 2000, the Open button in the Open dialog box has a drop-down list. From it, you can choose Open Read-Only or Open as Copy. Open Read-Only prevents changes from being saved to the presentation; Open as Copy creates a copy to be saved under a different name. Both of these help prevent inadvertent changes to a valuable presentation.

FINDING A PRESENTATION FILE

If you're having trouble locating your file, PowerPoint can help you look. Follow these steps to find a file:

1. Choose File, Open if the Open dialog box is not already open.

2. (Optional) If you know part of the name, use wildcards to indicate it. (See the following note.)

Wild Cards   You can use wild cards if you don't know the entire name of a file. The asterisk (*) wild-card character stands in for any character or set of characters, and the question mark (?) wild-card character stands in for any single character. For example, if you know the file begins with *P*, you could type P*.ppt to find all PowerPoint files that begin with *P*.

3. (Optional) If you want to look for a certain type of file, choose the type from the Files of type drop-down list.

4. Click the Tools button to open its menu, and choose Find. The Find dialog box appears. See Figure 6.4.

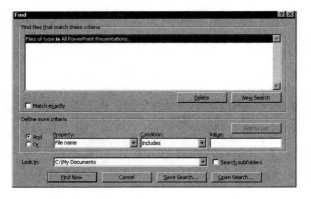

FIGURE 6.4   Use the Find dialog box to select the folders and drives you want to search.

5. In the Look in section at the bottom of the Find dialog box, narrow the search area as much as possible using these techniques:

- If you are sure the file is in a certain folder, type that folder's path (such as **C:\WINDOWS**) in the Look In box.

- If you are sure the file is on a certain drive, select that drive from the Look In drop-down list.

- If you don't know which drive contains the file, select My Computer from the Look In drop-down list.

6. Make sure the Search subfolders check box is marked. If it isn't, click it.

7. If you want to specify any other properties, do so like this:

   a. Open the Property drop-down list and choose a property. For example, to find a file that contains a certain word, choose Contents.

   b. Open the Condition drop-down list and choose a condition. Your choices vary depending on the property you chose.

   c. Type a value to match in the Value text box. For example, to find a file containing the name John Smith, type **John Smith**.

   d. Click the Add to List button.

8. Click the Find Now button. The File Open dialog box reappears and displays the files that match your search criteria.

9. Double-click the desired file to open it.

In this lesson, you learned how to save, close, open, and find presentations. In the next lesson, you learn how to print a presentation.

LESSON 7

PRINTING PRESENTATIONS, NOTES, AND HANDOUTS

In this lesson, you learn how to select a size and orientation for the slides in your presentation and how to print the slides, notes, and handouts you create.

 Notes and Handouts For instructions on how to create speaker's notes and audience handouts, see Lessons 23, "Creating Speaker's Notes," and 24, "Creating Audience Handouts."

QUICK PRINTING—NO OPTIONS

The quickest way to print is to use all the default settings. You don't get to make any decisions about your output, but you do get your printout without delay.

To print a quick copy, follow any of these steps:

- Click the Print button on the Standard toolbar.
- Choose File, Print, and click OK.
- Press Ctrl+P, and click OK.

When you use these methods for printing, you get a printout of your entire presentation in whatever view is onscreen and whatever pane is active. (To activate a pane, click it.) The following list describes what type of printout you can expect from each view:

- **Normal View, Slide Pane Active**   The entire presentation prints in Landscape orientation. Each slide fills an entire page.

- **Normal View, Outline Pane Active**   The entire outline prints in Portrait orientation.

- **Slide Sorter view**   The entire presentation prints in Portrait orientation with six slides per page.

- **Notes Pages view**   The entire presentation prints in Portrait orientation with one slide per page. Each slide prints with its notes beneath it.

 Orientation   The orientation setting tells the printer which edge of the paper should be at the "top" of the printout. If the top is across the wide edge, it's Landscape; if the top is across the narrow edge, it's Portrait.

CHANGING THE SLIDE SETUP

If you didn't get the printouts you expected from the previous procedure, you can change the selected presentation output, size, and orientation of the presentation in the Page Setup dialog box. To customize your printouts, follow these steps:

1. Choose File, Page Setup. The Page Setup dialog box appears onscreen, as shown in Figure 7.1.

2. Perform one of the following procedures to set the slide size:

   - To use a standard size, select a size from the Slides Sized For drop-down list. For example, you can have slides sized for regular 8×11 paper, 35mm slides, or an onscreen slide show.

   - To create a custom size, enter the dimensions in the Width and Height text boxes.

FIGURE 7.1   The Page Setup dialog box enables you to set the position and size of the slides on the page.

 Spin Boxes   The arrows to the right of the Width and Height text boxes enable you to adjust the settings in those boxes. Click the up arrow to increase the setting by .1 inch, or the down arrow to decrease it by .1 inch.

3. In the Number Slides From text box, type the number with which you want to start numbering slides. (This is usually 1, but you may want to start with a different number if the presentation is a continuation of another.)

4. Under the Slides heading, choose Portrait or Landscape orientation for your slides.

5. In the Notes, Handouts & Outline section, choose Portrait or Landscape for those items.

 Can I Print Notes and Handouts Differently?   If you want your notes printed in portrait orientation and your handouts printed in landscape orientation, just choose Portrait from the Notes, Handouts & Outline section of the Page Setup dialog box and print the notes. Then, before you print the handouts, go back to this dialog box and choose Landscape from the Notes, Handouts & Outline section.

6. Click OK. If you changed the orientation of your slides, you may have to wait a moment while PowerPoint repositions the slides.

CHOOSING WHAT AND HOW TO PRINT

If the default print options don't suit you, you can change them. Do you have more than one printer? If so, you can choose which printer to use. For example, you may want to use a color printer for overhead transparencies and a black-and-white printer for your handouts. You can also select options for printing multiple copies and for printing specific slides only.

To set your print options, follow these steps, and then print:

1. Choose File, Print. The Print dialog box appears, with the name of the currently selected printer in the Name box (see Figure 7.2).

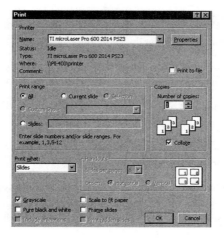

FIGURE 7.2   Choose your printing options in the Print dialog box.

2. If you want to use a different printer, open the Name drop-down list and select the printer you want.

Printer Properties   To make adjustments to your printer's settings, click the Properties button in the Print dialog box. The adjustments you can make vary from printer to printer, but you should be able to adjust graphics quality, select paper size, and choose which paper tray to use, among other things.

3. Choose what to print in the Print Range section:

- Choose All to print all the slides in the presentation.

- Choose Current Slide to print only the currently displayed slide.

- Enter a range of slide numbers in the Slides text box—for example, 2–4 to print slides 2, 3, and 4.

4. Open the Print What drop-down list and choose what you want to print. You can print slides, handouts, notes, or outlines.

5. If you want more than one copy, enter the number of copies you want in the Number of Copies box.

6. Select or deselect any of these check boxes in the dialog box as desired:

- Print to File   Select this option to send the output to a file rather than to your printer.

- Collate   If you are printing more than one copy, select this check box to collate (1, 2, 3, 1, 2, 3) each printed copy instead of printing all the copies of each page at once (1, 1, 2, 2, 3, 3).

- Grayscale   If you have a black-and-white printer, select this check box to make the color slides print more crisply. You also can select this check box to force a color printer to produce black-and-white output.

- Pure Black & White   This check box is like the preceding one, except everything prints in solid black and plain white, with no gray shading. This makes all slides look like line drawings.

- Scale to Fit Paper   If the slide (or whatever you're printing) is too large to fit on the page, select this check box to decrease the size of the slide to make it fit on the page. Now you won't have to paste two pieces of paper together to see the whole slide.

- Frame Slides   Select this check box if you want to print a border around each slide.

- Print Hidden Slides   If you have any hidden slides, you can choose whether to print them. If you don't have any hidden slides, this check box will be unavailable.

- Include Animations   If you have any animated elements on the slide, and you mark this check box, PowerPoint will do its best to approximate them in still form.

 Why Would I Print to File?   If you don't have the printer that you want to use hooked up to your computer, you can print to a file, and then take that file to the computer where the printer is. The other computer does not need to have PowerPoint installed on it to print PowerPoint documents.

7. Click OK to print.

In this lesson, you learned how to print slides, outlines, and notes, and how to set options for your printouts. In the next lesson, you learn how to change the overall appearance of the slides in a presentation.

LESSON 8
CHANGING A PRESENTATION'S LOOK

In this lesson, you learn various ways to give your presentation a professional and consistent look.

GIVING YOUR SLIDES A PROFESSIONAL LOOK

PowerPoint comes with dozens of professionally created designs you can apply to your presentations. These designs include background patterns, color choices, font choices, and more. When you apply a design template to your presentation, it applies its formatting to the Slide Master.

The Slide Master is not really a slide, but it looks like one. It is a design grid that you make changes to; these changes affect every slide in the presentation. When you apply a template, you are actually applying the template to the Slide Master, which in turn applies it to each slide.

There's another way to make global changes to an entire presentation: You can alter the Slide Master manually. For example, if you want a graphic to appear on every slide, you can place it on the Slide Master instead of pasting it onto each slide individually.

 Changing the Colors on a Single Slide   If you want to make some slides in the presentation look different from the others, you're in the wrong lesson. Check out Lesson 9, "Working with Presentation Colors and Backgrounds," to learn how to apply different color schemes to individual slides.

APPLYING A DIFFERENT DESIGN TEMPLATE

You can apply a different template to your presentation at any time, no matter how you originally created the presentation. To change the design template, follow these steps:

1. Choose Format, Apply Design Template. The Apply Design Template dialog box appears (see Figure 8.1).

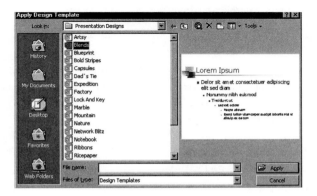

FIGURE 8.1   Choose a different template from the Apply Design Template dialog box.

2. Click the template name in the list. A sample of the template appears to the right of the list. If you do not see a sample area, click the Views button until it appears.

3. When you find the template you want to use, click Apply.

You can also apply any of the designs from the presentation templates that come with PowerPoint (that is, the templates that also include sample text). "Borrowing" the design from one of these templates does not insert any sample text; to get the sample text, you must start a new presentation based on one of those templates.

To access the presentation templates, click the Up One Level button in the Apply Design Template dialog box, and then double-click the Presentations folder to see a list of them.

USING AUTOLAYOUTS

While templates enable you to change the color and design of the presentation, AutoLayouts enable you to set the structure of a single slide. For example, if you want a graph and a picture on a slide, you can choose an AutoLayout that positions the two items for you.

If you prefer to place objects on your slide manually (without the placeholders provided by an AutoLayout), choose the Blank AutoLayout to create a blank slide, with no placeholders. Then place objects manually on the slide as you will learn to do in the upcoming lessons.

 Individual Slides? PowerPoint applies AutoLayouts to individual slides, but the template you choose and the Slide Master modifications you make affect the AutoLayouts too. This becomes more evident later in this lesson.

To use an AutoLayout, do the following:

1. In Normal, Outline, or Slide view, display the slide you want to change.

2. Choose Format, Slide Layout, or right-click the slide and choose Slide Layout from the shortcut menu. The Slide Layout dialog box appears (see Figure 8.2).

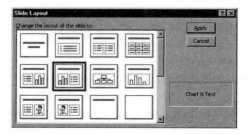

FIGURE 8.2   You can change an individual slide's layout with this dialog box.

3. Click the desired layout, or use the arrow keys to move the selection border to it.

4. Click the Apply button. PowerPoint applies the selected layout to the current slide.

EDITING THE SLIDE MASTER

Every presentation has a Slide Master that controls the overall appearance and layout of each slide. The Slide Master contains all the formatting information that the template brings to the presentation, such as colors and background patterns, and it also marks where the elements you use from the AutoLayout feature (such as text boxes) will appear on the slide.

To make changes to the Slide Master for your presentation, follow these steps:

1. Choose View, Master, Slide Master. Your Slide Master appears, as in Figure 8.3.

2. Make any changes to the Slide Master. (Anything you can do to a regular slide, you can do to a Slide Master.)

3. When you've finished working with the Slide Master, click the Close button (see Figure 8.3) to return to the view you started from.

The two most important elements on the Slide Master are the Title Area and Object Area for the AutoLayout objects. The Title Area contains the formatting specifications for each slide's title; that is, it tells PowerPoint the type size, style, and color to use for the text in the title of each slide. The Object Area contains the formatting specifications for all remaining text and AutoLayout objects on the slide.

 Slide Miniature   The Slide Miniature window enables you to see what the actual slides will look like in the presentation. The Slide Miniature window appears not only when you are working with the Slide Master, but also in other views where the entire slide may not be visible, such as Notes Page view.

Click here to exit
Slide Master view.   Title area   Object area   Slide Miniature window

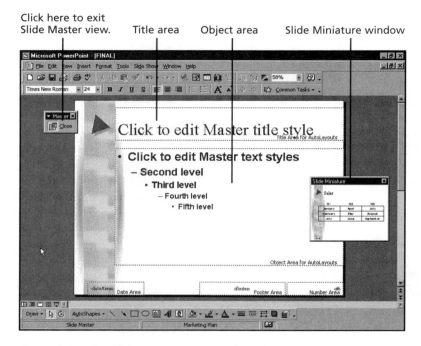

FIGURE 8.3   The Slide Master ensures that all slides in a presentation have a consistent look.

For most of PowerPoint's templates, the Object Area sets up specifications for a bulleted list, including the type of bullet, as well as the type styles, sizes, and indents for each item in the list.

In addition to the Title and Object Areas, the Slide Master can contain information about background colors, borders, page numbers, company logos, clip art objects, and any other elements you want to appear on every slide in the presentation.

In many ways, the Slide Master is like any other slide. In the following lessons, when you learn how to add text, graphics, borders, and other objects to a slide, keep in mind that you can add these objects on individual slides or on the Slide Master. When you add the object to the Slide Master, the object will appear on every slide.

In this lesson, you learned how to give your presentation a consistent look with templates and AutoLayouts. You also learned how to use the Slide Master to make global changes to your slides. In the next lesson, you learn how to change the color scheme and background design of a presentation.

LESSON 9

WORKING WITH PRESENTATION COLORS AND BACKGROUNDS

In this lesson, you learn how to change the color scheme and background design of a presentation to fine-tune your presentation's look. Each presentation design comes with a color scheme and background, but you may want to choose your own, while retaining the other presentation design settings.

UNDERSTANDING COLOR SCHEMES AND BACKGROUNDS

Color schemes are sets of professionally selected complementary colors that you can use as the primary colors of a presentation. Each color scheme controls the color of the background, lines, text, shadows, fills, and other items on a slide. Using one of these color schemes ensures that your presentation looks appealing and professional.

Backgrounds are solid colors, patterns, or textures that appear behind the objects on a slide.

You can select a color scheme and background for the Slide Master (which controls all the slides in the presentation), for the current slide, or for all slides in the presentation (thus overriding the Slide Master). Also, you can change individual colors in a color scheme to customize it.

SELECTING A COLOR SCHEME

The basic color scheme of your presentation depends on the active design template. You learned how to change design templates in Lesson 8, "Changing a Presentation's Look"—just select Format, Apply Design Template. Design templates include both color schemes and backgrounds.

Within each design template are several variations of one color scheme. All the color schemes in a template use the same basic colors, but each color scheme arranges its colors differently. For example, for onscreen viewing, the color scheme is a dark background and light text; for printing on a color printer, a light background and dark text; and for printing on a one-color printer, a black-and-white color scheme.

You can select a color scheme for one slide or for all the slides in your presentation. To select a color scheme, perform the following steps:

1. If you don't want to change all the slides in the presentation, display or select the slide(s) with the color scheme you want to change.

2. Choose Format, Slide Color Scheme. The Color Scheme dialog box appears.

3. Click the Standard tab if it's not displayed. The color schemes available for the current design template appear (see Figure 9.1).

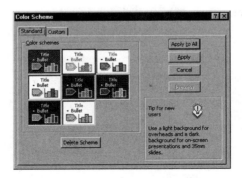

FIGURE 9.1 You can choose a standard color scheme from the ones the current template offers.

4. Click one of the color schemes, and click Apply to apply it to the selected slides or Apply All to apply it to all slides in the presentation.

CUSTOMIZING A COLOR SCHEME

Even though each template comes with its own color scheme, you can customize the scheme for a presentation. You can adjust individual colors, or radically change them all.

 Stay Consistent Be careful when you change the colors on a single slide. You don't want one slide to clash with the rest of your slides.

Follow these steps to customize a color scheme:

1. If you don't want to change all the slides in the presentation, display or select the slide with the color scheme you want to change.

2. Choose Format, Slide Color Scheme. The Color Scheme dialog box appears.

3. Click the Custom tab. The dialog box changes, as shown in Figure 9.2.

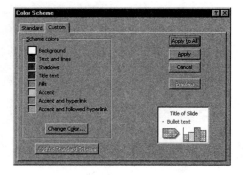

FIGURE 9.2 You can change individual colors in a scheme with the Custom tab.

4. Click one of the colors (for example, Background), and click the Change Color button. A dialog box appears that enables you to select a new color. For example, the Background Color dialog box is shown in Figure 9.3.

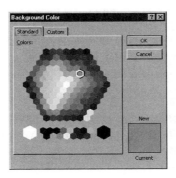

FIGURE 9.3   Each onscreen element has its own dialog box for customizing its color.

5. To select a color, click the Standard tab, click any color you see, and click OK. To create a new color, click the Custom tab, use the controls to custom select a color, and click OK.

Custom Controls Most beginners use the Standard tab in step 5. There are enough colors shown there to suit most purposes. With the custom controls, you can fine-tune a color's hue, saturation, and luminescence, and adjust its red, green, and blue tones numerically.

6. Repeat steps 4 and 5 for each color you want to change.

7. Click Apply to All to apply the new colors to every slide in the presentation, or click Apply to apply them to only the current slide.

More Background Controls You can change the color of the background using the Format, Slide Color Scheme command. If you want to change the texture or pattern of the background, or use a picture as a background, you need to use the Format, Background command, discussed later in this lesson.

COPYING A SLIDE'S COLOR SCHEME TO ANOTHER SLIDE

If you want to change the color scheme for an entire presentation, it's best to make the changes to the Slide Master. However, if you want to change several slides, but not all of them, you can make the changes to a single slide and copy that slide's color scheme to the others. Follow these steps to copy a slide's color scheme:

1. Display your presentation in Slide Sorter view.

2. Select the slide containing the color scheme you want to copy.

3. Click the Format Painter button on the toolbar.

4. Click the slide that you want to receive the color scheme.

5. Repeat the process to recolor each slide you want to change.

CHANGING THE BACKGROUND DESIGN

An effective background adds a professional look to any presentation. PowerPoint enables you to set the background to any color, and to add patterns, textures, and shadings to it.

PowerPoint on the Web If you are creating a presentation for use on the Web, try to keep the background light-colored. It will be easier for your readers to view on their monitors this way. Save dark backgrounds for slides designed to be shown on large screens.

To change the background for your presentation or to modify the existing background, perform the following steps:

1. Display or select the slide with the background you want to change. To change the slide backgrounds in the entire presentation, display the Slide Master.

2. Choose Format, Background or right-click the background and select Background from the shortcut menu. The Background dialog box appears.

3. Open the drop-down list under Background Fill (see Figure 9.4).

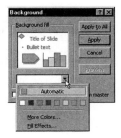

FIGURE 9.4 Choose a color from the ones shown, or click More Colors or Fill Effects.

4. Click one of the following options:

   - Automatic sets the background to whatever the Slide Master currently shows as the background.

   A solid color sets the background to that color.

   - More Colors opens a Colors dialog box similar to the one shown in Figure 9.3, in which you can choose from a color assortment.

   - Fill Effects opens a dialog box in which you can choose many special effects such as a gradient fill, textured backgrounds, or pictures used as backgrounds.

Gradient Fill A gradient begins the background with one color at the top of the slide and gradually changes to another color. When one of those colors is white (or in some schemes black), it's known as a one-color gradient. When neither color is white (or black), it's a two-color gradient.

5. Click Apply to apply the background only to this slide, or click Apply To All to apply the background to all the slides in the presentation.

In this lesson, you learned how to select and modify a color scheme, and how to copy a color scheme from one presentation to another. You also learned how to change the background color and design for a slide or presentation. In the next lesson, you learn how to insert, delete, and copy slides.

LESSON 10

INSERTING, DELETING, AND COPYING SLIDES

In this lesson, you learn how to insert new slides, delete slides, and copy slides in a presentation.

INSERTING A SLIDE

You can insert a slide into a presentation at any time and in any position in the presentation. To insert a slide, follow these steps:

1. Select the slide that appears just before the place where you want to insert the new slide. (You can select the slide in any view.)

 2. Choose Insert, New Slide, click the New Slide button, or press Ctrl+M. The New Slide dialog box appears (see Figure 10.1).

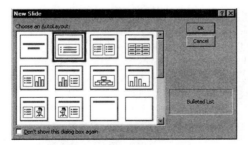

FIGURE **10.1** In the New Slide dialog box, you can choose a layout for the slide you're inserting.

3. In the Choose an AutoLayout list, click a slide layout, or use the arrow keys to highlight it.

4. Click the OK button. PowerPoint inserts a slide that has the specified layout (see Figure 10.2).

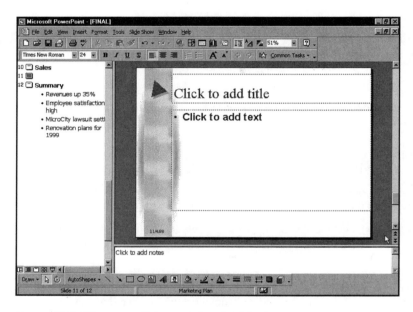

FIGURE 10.2 The new slide contains the blank structure you selected; you supply the content.

5. Follow the directions indicated on the slide layout to add text or other objects. For text boxes, you click an area to select it and then you type in your text. For other object placeholders, you double-click the placeholder.

 Cloning a Slide To create an exact replica of a slide (in any view), select the slide you want to duplicate. Then select Insert, Duplicate Slide. The new slide is inserted after the original slide. You can move the slide anywhere you want.

ADDING SLIDES FROM ANOTHER PRESENTATION

If you want to insert some or all of the slides from another presentation into the current presentation, perform these steps:

1. Open the presentation into which you want to insert the slides.

2. Select the slide located before the position where you want to insert the slides.

3. Choose Insert, Slides from Files. The Slide Finder dialog box appears.

4. Click the Browse button to display the Browse dialog box.

5. Change the drive or folder if needed. (Refer to the section "Changing the Drive or Folder" in Lesson 6, "Saving, Closing, Opening, and Finding Presentations.")

6. Double-click the name of the presentation that contains the slides you want to insert into the open presentation.

7. Click the Display button. The slides from the presentation appear in the Slide Finder window (see Figure 10.3).

Click here to view the slides as a list with a preview window.

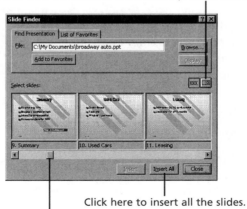

Click here to insert all the slides.

Use this scrollbar to move through the slides.

FIGURE **10.3** You can select any or all of the slides from the selected presentation to add to the open presentation.

View the Slides in a Different Way You can click this button if you prefer to see a list of the slide titles instead of three slides at a time. When you click the button, the display changes to a list of titles on the left and a preview window on the right that displays the selected slide.

8. Click the slides you want to insert and then click the Insert button. If you want to insert all the slides, click the Insert All button.

9. When you are finished inserting slides, click the Close button. The inserted slides appear right after the slide that was selected in step 2.

Make a Favorites List If there is a presentation that you regularly use to insert slides from, you can add it to your Favorites List by clicking the Add to Favorites button in the Find Slides dialog box. Then the next time you want to insert slides from that presentation, just click the List of Favorites tab in the Find Slides dialog box and select the presentation from the list. You might, for example, have a presentation that contains some standard slides that you include in every presentation for a certain audience.

CREATING SLIDES FROM A DOCUMENT OUTLINE

If you have a word processing document with outline-style headings in it, PowerPoint can pull the headings from the document and use the headings to create slides with bulleted lists. To create slides from a document outline:

1. Choose Insert, Slides from Outline. The Insert Outline dialog box appears.

2. Use the Insert Outline dialog box to locate the document file you want to use. (Refer to "Changing the Drive or Folder" in Lesson 6 if you need help locating the file.)

3. Double-click the name of the document file.

SELECTING SLIDES

In the following sections, you learn to delete, copy, and move slides. However, before you can do anything with a slide, you have to select it. To select slides, follow these directions:

- To select a single slide, click it.

- To select two or more neighboring slides in the Outline pane, click the first slide, and then hold down the Shift key while clicking the last slide in the group.

- To select multiple contiguous slides in Slide Sorter view, click in front of the first slide and then hold down the mouse button and drag to the last slide. All slides that fall in between become selected (see Figure 10.4).

 Don't Drag the Slide If you are trying to select multiple contiguous slides, drag from in front of the first slide. Don't start dragging while pointing directly at the first slide because it will move and fail to highlight the remaining slides that you want to select.

- To select two or more non-neighboring slides (in Slide Sorter view only), hold down the Ctrl key while clicking on each slide. You cannot select non-neighboring slides in other views.

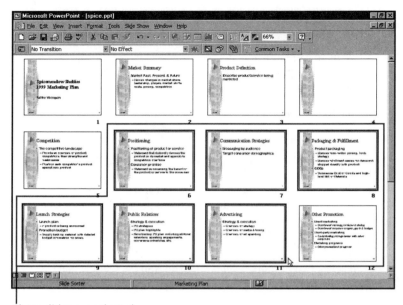

These slides are selected.

FIGURE 10.4   You can select a block of slides in Slide Sorter view by dragging from the first one to the last one.

DELETING SLIDES

You can delete a slide from any view. To delete a slide, perform the following steps:

1. Select the slide you want to delete. You can delete multiple slides by displaying or selecting more than one slide.

2. Choose Edit, Delete Slide. The slide disappears.

Quicker Deleting   On the Outline or in Slide Sorter view, you can just select the slides you want to delete and press the Delete key on the keyboard.

Oops!   If you delete a slide by mistake, you can get it back by selecting Edit, Undo, by pressing Ctrl+Z, or by clicking the Undo button on the Standard toolbar.

CUTTING, COPYING, AND PASTING SLIDES

You can use the cut, copy, and paste features to copy and move slides, either in the same presentation or into other presentations. To cut (or copy) a slide and paste it in a presentation, perform the following steps:

1. Change to Slide Sorter view, or display Normal view and work with the Outline pane.

2. Select the slide(s) you want to copy or cut.

3. Open the Edit menu, and select Cut or Copy to either move or copy the slide(s) to the Windows Clipboard, or use the Copy or Cut toolbar button.

 Windows Clipboard The Windows Clipboard is a temporary holding area for cut or copied items. You can cut or copy items to the Clipboard and then paste them on a slide, or cut or copy an entire slide or group of slides.

 Quick Cut or Copy To bypass the Edit menu, press Ctrl+C to copy or Ctrl+X to cut, or click the Cut or Copy button on the Standard toolbar.

4. If you want to paste the slide(s) into a different presentation, open that presentation.

5. In Slide Sorter view, select the slide after which you want to place the cut or copied slide(s), or on the Outline pane, move the insertion point to the end of the text in the slide after which you want to insert the cut or copied slide(s).

6. Choose Edit, Paste or press Ctrl+V. (You can also click the Paste button on the Standard toolbar.) PowerPoint inserts the cut or copied slides.

Drag and Drop   Although it's primarily used for moving slides, drag-and-drop can also be used for copying them in Slide Sorter view. You just drag a slide where you want the copy to go, holding down the Ctrl key as you drag.

In this lesson, you learned how to insert, delete, cut, copy, and paste slides. In the next lesson, you learn how to add text to a slide.

LESSON 11
ADDING TEXT TO A SLIDE

In this lesson, you learn how to add text to a slide and change the text alignment and line spacing.

CREATING A TEXT BOX

As you have learned in previous lessons, you can put text on a slide by typing text in Outline view or filling in the placeholders on an AutoLayout (see Lesson 8, "Changing a Presentation's Look"). However, these methods both provide fairly generic results. If you want to type additional text on a slide, you must first create a text box.

 Text Box A text box acts as a receptacle for the text. Text boxes often contain bulleted lists, notes, and labels (used to point to important parts of illustrations).

To create a text box, perform the following steps:

1. Switch to Normal or Slide view. (Refer to Lesson 5, "Working with Slides in Different Views," for help with views.)

2. If you want the text box to appear on a new slide, insert a slide into the presentation. (Choose Insert, New Slide; see Lesson 10, "Inserting, Deleting, and Copying Slides," for details.)

3. Click the Text Box button on the Drawing toolbar.

4. Click the slide where you want the text box to appear. A small text box appears (see Figure 11.1). (It will expand as needed as you type in it.)

Text you type will appear here.

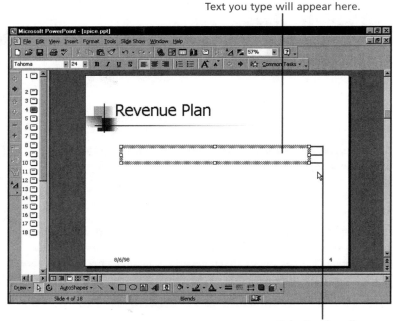

Selection handles

FIGURE 11.1   You can enter text in the text box.

5. Type the text that you want to appear in the text box. Press Enter to start a new paragraph. Don't worry if the text box becomes too wide; you can resize it after you are done typing.

6. When you are done, click anywhere outside the text box to see how the text will appear on the finished slide.

7. If desired, drag the text box's selection handles to resize it. If you make the box narrower, text within a paragraph may wrap to the next line.

If the text does not align correctly in the text box, see "Changing the Text Alignment and Line Spacing" later in this lesson to learn how to change it.

Framing a Text Box The border that appears around a text box when you create or select it does not appear on the printed slide. To add a border that does print, see Lesson 20, "Formatting Objects".

SELECTING, DELETING, AND MOVING A TEXT BOX

If you go back and click anywhere inside the text box, a selection box appears around it. If you click the selection box border, handles appear around the text box, as shown in Figure 11.1. You can drag the box's border to move the box, or drag a handle to resize it. PowerPoint wraps the text automatically as needed to fit inside the box.

To delete a text box, select it (so handles appear around it), and then press the Delete key.

EDITING TEXT IN A TEXT BOX

To edit text in a text box, first click anywhere inside the text box to select it; then, perform any of the following steps:

- To select text, drag the I-beam pointer over the text you want to select. (To select a single word, double-click it. To select an entire paragraph, triple-click.)

 Auto Word Select When you drag over text, PowerPoint selects whole words. If you want to select individual characters, select Tools, Options, click the Edit tab, and deselect the When selecting, automatically select entire word check box.

- To delete text, select the text and press the Delete key. You can also use the Delete or Backspace keys to delete single characters to the right or left of the insertion point, respectively.

- To insert text, click the I-beam pointer where you want to insert the text and type.

- To replace text, select the text you want to replace and type the new text. When you start typing, PowerPoint deletes the selected text.

- To copy and paste text, select the text you want to copy and choose Edit, Copy, click the Copy button on the Standard toolbar, or press Ctrl+C. Move the insertion point to where you want the text pasted (it can be in a different text box) and choose Edit, Paste, click the Paste button, or press Ctrl+V.

- To cut and paste (move) text, select the text you want to cut and choose Edit, Cut, click the Cut button on the Standard toolbar, or press Ctrl+X. Move the insertion point to where you want the text pasted (it can be in a different text box), and choose Edit, Paste, click the Paste button, or press Ctrl+V.

CHANGING THE TEXT ALIGNMENT AND LINE SPACING

When you first type text, PowerPoint automatically sets it against the left edge of the text box. To change the paragraph alignment, perform the following steps:

1. Click anywhere inside the paragraph you want to realign.

2. Select Format, Alignment. The Alignment submenu appears.

3. Select Left, Center, Right, or Justify, to align the paragraph as desired (see Figure 11.2 for examples).

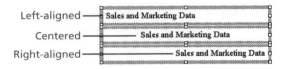

FIGURE 11.2   You can align each paragraph in a text box.

Some Alignment Shortcuts To quickly set left alignment, press Ctrl+L or click the Align Left button on
the Formatting toolbar. To quickly apply centered
alignment, press Ctrl+C or click the Center button. To
quickly apply right alignment, press Ctrl+R or click the
Align Right button.

The default setting for line spacing is single-space. To change the line spacing in a paragraph, perform these steps:

1. Click inside the paragraph you want to change, or select all the paragraphs you want to change.

2. Select Format, Line Spacing. The Line Spacing dialog box appears, as shown in Figure 11.3.

FIGURE 11.3 The Line Spacing dialog box.

3. Click the arrow buttons to the right of any of the following text boxes to change the line spacing:

   Line Spacing This setting controls the space between the lines in a paragraph.

   Before Paragraph This setting controls the space between this paragraph and the paragraph that comes before it.

   After Paragraph This setting controls the space between this paragraph and the paragraph that comes after it.

4. Click OK.

Lines or Points? The drop-down list box that appears to the right of each setting allows you to set the line spacing in lines or points. A line is the current line height (based on text size). A point is a unit commonly used to measure text and is approximately 1/72 of an inch.

ADDING A WORDART OBJECT

PowerPoint comes with an auxiliary program called WordArt that can help you create graphic text effects. To insert a WordArt object into a slide, perform the following steps:

1. Display the slide on which you want to place the WordArt object in Slide view.

2. Click the WordArt button on the Drawing toolbar (at the bottom of the screen). The WordArt Gallery dialog box appears, showing many samples of WordArt types.

3. Click the sample that best represents the WordArt type you want, and then click OK. The Edit WordArt Text dialog box appears (see Figure 11.4).

FIGURE **11.4** Enter the text, size, and font to be used into the Edit WordArt Text dialog box.

4. Choose a font and size from the respective drop-down lists.

5. Type the text you want to use in the Text box.

6. Click OK. PowerPoint creates the WordArt text on your slide, as shown in Figure 11.5.

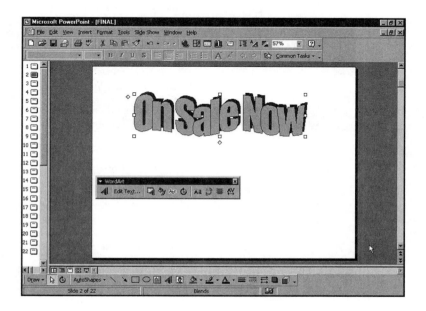

FIGURE **11.5**   Here is some finished WordArt on a slide. Notice the WordArt toolbar below it.

After you have created some WordArt, you have access to the WordArt toolbar, shown in Figure 11.5. You can use it to modify your WordArt. Table 11.1 summarizes the toolbar's buttons.

TABLE 11.1 BUTTONS ON THE WORDART TOOLBAR

BUTTON	NAME	PURPOSE
	Insert WordArt	Creates a new WordArt object
None	Edit Text	Edits the text, size, and font of the selected WordArt object
	WordArt Gallery	Changes the type of the current WordArt object
	Format WordArt	Opens a Format WordArt dialog box
	WordArt Shape	Changes the WordArt shape
	Free Rotate	Rotates the WordArt object
	WordArt Same Letter Heights	Makes all the letters the same height
	WordArt Vertical Text	Changes between vertical and horizontal text orientation
	WordArt Alignment	Changes the text alignment
	WordArt Character Spacing	Changes the spacing between letters

To edit the WordArt object, double-click it to display the WordArt toolbar and text entry box. Enter your changes, and then click outside the WordArt object. You can move the object by dragging its border or resize it by dragging a handle.

In this lesson, you learned how to add text to a slide, change the text alignment and spacing, and add WordArt objects. In the next lesson, you learn how to use tables and tabs to create columns and lists.

LESSON 12

CREATING COLUMNS AND LISTS

In this lesson, you learn how to use tabs to create columns of text, bulleted lists, numbered lists, and other types of lists.

WORKING IN MULTIPLE COLUMNS

If you need multiple columns of text, you have several options:

- You can use separate text boxes. The easiest way is to use the two-column AutoLayout, which includes two automatic text boxes, but you can also create text boxes manually. (AutoLayouts are described in Lesson 8, "Changing a Presentation's Look," and manual text boxes in Lesson 11, "Adding Text to a Slide.")

- You can place tab stops in a single text box, and press Tab to create columns.

- You can use a table to create a grid.

In this lesson, you learn how to do all three of these things.

CREATING COLUMNS WITH AN AUTOLAYOUT

The easiest way to create columns of text is to use an AutoLayout that contains one or more text boxes. The default AutoLayout is a single bulleted list, but you can change to a double-column list by changing the slide's AutoLayout as described in Lesson 8. (Hint: use the Format, Slide Layout command.)

When you use the two-column AutoLayout, the columns appear on the Outline pane as 1 and 2, as shown in Figure 12.1.

Pane 1 text

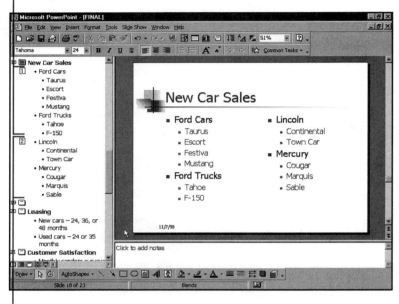

Pane 2 text

FIGURE 12.1   A two-column AutoLayout provides two panes in which to enter text.

USING TABS TO CREATE COLUMNS

You can also create multiple columns using tab stops. To set the tabs for a multicolumn list, perform the following steps:

1. Open the presentation and view the slide you want to work with in Slide view.

2. Create a text box for the text if one does not already exist. (For instructions on how to create a text box, see Lesson 11.)

Disappearing text box   If you are creating a brand-new, manual text box in step 2, type a few characters in it to "anchor" it so it does not disappear when you click outside it. Then resize it to the final size you want by dragging its left and right selection handles. You should make the text box its final size before you set the tabs.

3. Click anywhere inside the text box for which you want to set the tabs.

4. If you already typed text inside the text box, select the text.

5. Select View, Ruler to display the ruler, if it does not already appear.

6. Click the Tab button at the left end of the ruler until it represents the type of tab you want to set. See Table 12.1.

7. Click each place in the ruler where you want to set the selected type of tab stop, as shown in Figure 12.2.

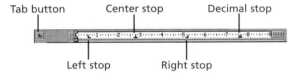

FIGURE **12.2**   The ruler lets you enter and change tab stop settings.

8. Repeat steps 4 and 5 if you want to set different types of tab stops at different positions.

9. To change the position of an existing tab stop setting, drag it on the ruler to the desired position. To delete an existing tab stop setting, drag it off the ruler.

10. (Optional) To turn off the ruler, select View, Ruler.

TABLE 12.1 TAB BUTTON STOP TYPES

BUTTON APPEARANCE	TAB STOP TYPE
	Aligns the left end of the line against the tab stop.
	Centers the text on the tab stop.
	Aligns the right end of the line against the tab stop.
	Aligns the tab stop on a period. This is called a decimal tab and is useful for aligning a column of numbers that uses decimal points.

Don't Forget the Slide Master! Throughout this lesson, keep in mind that you can enter your changes on the Slide Master or on individual slides. If you change the Slide Master, the change affects all slides in the presentation. For details on displaying the Slide Master, see Lesson 8.

CREATING A TABLE

The easiest way to create a table on a slide is to use the Table AutoLayout. Change the slide to that AutoLayout (Format, Slide Layout), and then double-click the table placeholder to create a table.

The other way to add a table is with the Insert, Table command. Follow these steps:

1. Display the slide on which you want to place the table.

2. Choose Insert, Table. The Insert Table dialog box appears.

3. Enter the number of columns you want in the Number of Columns text box.

4. Enter the number of rows in the Number of Rows text box.

5. Click OK. The table appears, and the mouse pointer looks like a pencil.

6. Press Esc. The mouse pointer becomes normal again, and you are ready to work with the table. See Figure 12.3.

Drag the line beneath a row or to the right of a column to resize it individually.

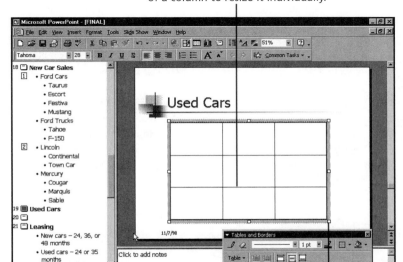

Drag a selection handle to resize the table overall.

FIGURE 12.3 Type in the table cells, creating multiple columns.

After you have a table on a slide, you can work with it like this:

• Click inside a table cell and type. You can move from cell to cell by pressing Tab to go forward or Shift+Tab to go back.

• If you need to resize the table, drag a selection handle, just as you would with any object.

- To adjust the row height or column width, position the mouse pointer on a line between two rows or columns and drag.

- To change the borders around the cells, select the cells you want to work with and then use the buttons on the Drawing toolbar to adjust the thickness, color, and style of the table gridlines.

You can do much more to format a table than I can tell you here. For more information, consult the PowerPoint Help system.

Invisible Table   To make a table appear to be multiple columns of untabular text, turn off all the gridlines in the table. To do so, select all the cells in the table. Then right-click and choose Borders and Fill. In the Format Table dialog box that appears, click each of the border buttons to turn the border off for each side of each cell in the table. Click OK to finish up.

WORKING WITH BULLETED LISTS

When you enter new slides on the Outline pane, the default layout is a simple bulleted list. If you've done this, you've already created a bulleted list. You can turn off the bullets in front of any paragraphs by selecting the paragraphs and clicking the Bullets button on the Formatting toolbar to toggle the bullet off.

When you create your own text boxes without relying on an AutoLayout, the text does not have bullets by default. You can add your own bullets by following these steps:

1. Click inside the paragraph you want to transform into a bulleted list, or select one or more paragraphs.

2. Select Format, Bullets and Numbering. The Bullets and Numbering dialog box appears.

Quick Bullets To bypass the dialog box, simply click the Bullets button on the Formatting toolbar to insert a bullet, or right-click and select Bullet from the shortcut menu. You can click the Bullets button again to remove the bullet.

3. Select the bullet style you want (see Figure 12.4).

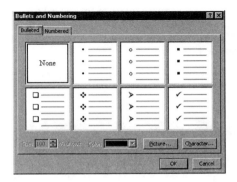

FIGURE 12.4 Choose the bullet character you want from the several samples provided.

4. Click OK. PowerPoint transforms the selected text into a bulleted list. (If you press Enter at the end of a bulleted paragraph, the next paragraph starts with a bullet.)

More Bullet Options You can choose a different bullet character than the seven samples shown in Figure 12.4. Just click the Character button to select another character from any font, or click the Picture button to choose a picture as a bullet. You can also select a Size and Color for the bullet using the Size and Color controls in the Bullets and Numbering dialog box.

WORKING WITH NUMBERED LISTS

Numbered lists are just like bulleted ones, except they have sequential numbers instead of symbols. You can convert any paragraphs to a numbered list by selecting them and clicking the Numbering button on the Formatting toolbar. Select the paragraphs again and click the Numbering button again to toggle the numbering off.

You can also create numbered lists with the Bullets and Numbering dialog box, just as you did with bullets. Follow these steps:

1. Select the paragraphs that you want to convert to a numbered list.

2. Choose Format, Bullets and Numbering.

3. Click the Numbered tab. The numbered list styles appear. See Figure 12.5.

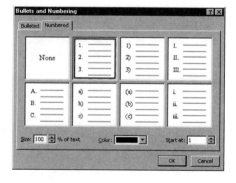

FIGURE 12.5   Choose the numbering style you want, or turn numbering off by choosing None.

4. Click the style you want for your list.

5. (Optional) Change the Size or Color of the numbers.

6. (Optional) If you want the list to start at a number other than 1, enter it in the Start At text box.

7. Click OK.

In this lesson, you learned how to create columns with AutoLayouts, tabs, and tables, and how to work with bulleted lists. In the next lesson, you learn how to change the style, size, and color of text.

LESSON 13
CHANGING THE LOOK OF YOUR TEXT

In this lesson, you learn how to change the appearance of text by changing its font, style, size, and color.

FORMATTING TEXT WITH THE FONT DIALOG BOX

You can enhance your text by using the Font dialog box or by using various tools on the Formatting toolbar. Use the Font dialog box if you want to add several enhancements to your text at one time. Use the Formatting toolbar to add one enhancement at a time.

 Fonts, Styles, and Effects In PowerPoint, a *font* is a family of text that has the same design or typeface (for example, Arial or Courier). A *style* is a standard enhancement, such as bold or italic. An *effect* is a special enhancement, such as shadow or underline.

You can change the font of existing text or of text you are about to type by performing the following steps:

1. To change the font of existing text, select text by dragging the I-beam pointer over the text.

2. Choose Format, Font. The Font dialog box appears, as shown in Figure 13.1.

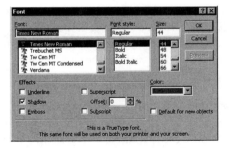

FIGURE 13.1   You can select a font in the Font dialog box.

 Right-Click Quick You can right-click the text and select Font from the shortcut menu instead of performing steps 1 and 2.

3. From the Font list, select the font you want to use.

 TrueType Fonts The TT to the left of a font name identifies the font as a TrueType font. TrueType fonts are *scalable*, which means you can set them at any point size. When you save a presentation, you can choose to embed TrueType fonts so you can display or print the font on any computer whether or not it has that font installed.

4. From the Font Style list, select any style you want to apply to the text. (To remove styles from text, select Regular.)

5. From the Size list, select any size in the list, or type a size directly into the box. (With TrueType fonts, you can type any point size, even sizes that do not appear on the list.)

6. In the Effects group, select any special effects you want to add to the text, such as Underline, Shadow, or Emboss. You can also choose Superscript or Subscript, though these are less common.

7. To change the color of your text, click the arrow button to the right of the Color list, and click the desired color. (For more colors, click the More Colors option at the bottom of the Color drop-down list and use the dialog box that appears to select a color.)

 Changing the Background Color Each presentation has its own color scheme, which includes background and text colors. You learned about creating and changing color schemes in Lesson 9, "Working with Presentation Colors and Backgrounds."

8. Click OK to apply the new look to your text. (If you selected text before styling it, the text appears in the new style. If you did not select text, any text you type appears in the new style.)

 Title and Object Area Text If you change a font on an individual slide, the font change applies only to that slide. To change the font for *all* the slides in the presentation, you need to change the font on the Slide Master (see Lesson 8, "Changing a Presentation's Look"). To change the Slide Master, select View, Master, Slide Master. Select a text area and perform the preceding steps to change the look of the text on all slides.

FORMATTING TEXT WITH THE FORMATTING TOOLBAR

As shown in Figure 13.2, the Formatting toolbar contains several tools for changing the font, size, style, and color of text.

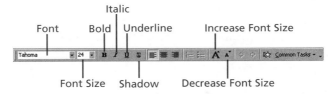

FIGURE 13.2 The Formatting toolbar contains several tools for styling text.

To use the tools, follow these steps:

1. To change the look of existing text, select the text.

2. To change fonts, open the Font drop-down list (see Figure 13.2) and click the desired font.

3. To change font size, open the Font Size drop-down list (shown in Figure 13.2) and click the desired size, or type a size directly into the box.

 Incrementing the Type Size To increase or decrease the text size to the next size up or down, click the Increase Font Size or Decrease Font Size buttons on the Formatting toolbar.

4. To add a style or effect to the text (bold, italic, underline, or shadow), click the appropriate button(s):

 Bold

Italic

Underline

Shadow

CHANGING FONT COLOR

As you have already seen, you can change the font color through the Font dialog box. You can also change it with the Font Color button on the Drawing toolbar (at the bottom of the screen). Just do the following:

1. Select the text for which you want to change the color.

2. Click the down-pointing arrow next to the Font Color button on the Drawing toolbar. A menu of options appears (see Figure 13.3).

Click one of these preselected colors to stay within the presentation design's color scheme.

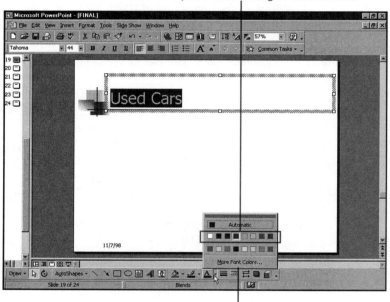

Or click here for more choices.

FIGURE 13.3 When you click the arrow next to the Font Colors button, this menu of options appears.

3. Do one of the following:

- Click one of the colored blocks on the top row to change
the font to one of the prechosen colors for the presentation
design you're using.

- Click a colored block on the second row to change to
another color that you have already used elsewhere in the
presentation (besides the prechosen ones).

- Click the More Font Colors option to display a Colors dialog box, click a color in that box, and click OK.

COPYING TEXT FORMATS

If your presentation contains text with a format you want to use, you can
pick up the format from the existing text and apply it to other text. To
copy text formats, perform the following steps:

1. Highlight the text with the format you want to use.

2. Click the Format Painter button on the toolbar. PowerPoint
copies the format.

3. Drag the mouse pointer across the text to which you want to
apply the format.

In this lesson, you learned how to change the appearance of text by
changing its font, size, style, and color. You also learned how to copy text
formats. In the next lesson, you learn how to check your work for misspellings and how to find and replace text.

LESSON 14
OTHER EDITING TOOLS

In this lesson, you learn how to check your presentation for spelling errors, and to find and replace text in all presentation materials.

CHECKING FOR MISSPELLINGS AND TYPOS

PowerPoint uses a built-in dictionary to spell check your entire presentation, including all slides, outlines, notes and handout pages, and all four master views. To check the spelling in your presentation, perform the following steps:

1. Click the Spelling button on the Standard toolbar (Alternatively, select Tools, Spelling, or press F7.)

    If there are no misspellings, PowerPoint displays a dialog box saying that the spell check is complete. Click OK to close it.

    If a misspelling is found, the Spelling dialog box appears, displaying the first questionable word with all the options for handling it (see Figure 14.1).

FIGURE **14.1** The Spelling dialog box displays the questionable word and suggests corrections.

2. For the word that the spell checker found, select one of these options:

- Ignore—Skips only this occurrence of the word.

- Ignore All—Ignores every occurrence of the word.

- Change—Replaces only this occurrence of the word with the word in the Change To box. (You can type a correction in the Change To box or select a correct spelling from the Suggestions list.)

- Change All—Replaces every occurrence of the word with the word in the Change To box. (To insert an entry in the Change To box, type it, or select an entry from the Suggestions list.)

- Add—Adds the word to the dictionary, so the spell checker will not question it again.

- Suggest—Displays a list of suggested words, if suggestions do not appear already.

- AutoCorrect—Adds the misspelled word to the AutoCorrect list, with the word that appears in the Change To box as its correction. From then on, PowerPoint will automatically correct that misspelling if you make it again.

- Close—Closes the Spelling dialog box.

3. Repeat step 2 until the spell checker finishes checking the presentation. When the spell checker finishes, a dialog box appears to tell you that spell check is complete.

4. Click OK.

 Spell Check On-the-Fly You can also correct spelling word-by-word as you type. When you see a word with a wavy red underline, right-click it for a pop-up list of spelling suggestions, and then click the correct spelling to make the correction immediately.

EDITING THE AUTOCORRECT LIST

There are certain misspellings that many people commonly make, such as transposing letters ("teh" instead of "the") and leaving out letters or apostrophes ("ther" or "youre"). AutoCorrect can identify and correct these common errors for you automatically. And, as you saw in the Spelling dialog box (see Figure 14.1), you can add your own common errors to the list, too.

To view and make changes to the list of AutoCorrected words, follow these steps. Choose Tools, AutoCorrect. The AutoCorrect dialog box opens (see Figure 14.2).

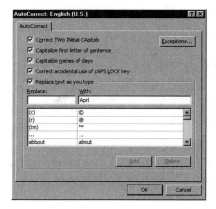

FIGURE 14.2   You can edit the list of AutoCorrected words from this dialog box.

From here, you can do any of the following:

- (Optional) Deselect any of the check boxes at the top of the dialog box to turn off any AutoCorrect features you don't want to use.

- To add a correction to the list, type the misspelling in the Replace text box and the correction in the With text box, and click the Add button.

- To remove a correction from the list, scroll through the list to find it, highlight it, and click the Delete button.

- To make a change to a correction, highlight it, make the change in the Replace or With text boxes, and click the Replace button.

When you're finished making changes to the AutoCorrect list, click OK.

Why Would I Delete an AutoCorrection? In most cases, you will want to leave all the check boxes marked and the corrections in place on the list. However, sometimes a special situation requires you to turn off a correction. For instance, my publisher's editors use (c) to indicate a heading, so I had to delete the AutoCorrect entry that changed (c) to a copyright symbol.

FINDING AND REPLACING TEXT

If you want to find a particular word or phrase in your presentation, but you can't remember where it is, you can have PowerPoint find the word or phrase for you. You can also have PowerPoint search for a word or phrase and replace one or all instances of the word or phrase.

To search for specific text, perform the following steps:

1. Choose Edit, Find, or press Ctrl+F. The Find dialog box appears (see Figure 14.3).

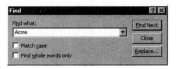

FIGURE 14.3 Use the Find dialog box to find all occurrences of a particular word or phrase.

2. In the Find What text box, type the word or phrase you want to search for in the text.

3. (Optional) Select either or both of the following options:

- Match Case—Finds text that matches the capitalization in the Find What text box. For example, if you type Widget, the search skips widget.

- Find Whole Words Only—Skips any occurrences of the text that appear in a part of another word. For example, if you type book, the search skips bookkeeper.

4. Click the Find Next button. PowerPoint finds next occurrence of the word and highlights it.

 Editing and Formatting Text To edit or format text, simply perform the operation as you would under normal circumstances. The Find dialog box remains onscreen as you work.

5. When you've found all occurrences, PowerPoint displays a message to that effect. Click OK to close the message. To close the Find dialog box before you have found all occurrences, click the Close button.

 Quick Jump to Replace If you start out using Find and then realize that you want to replace the found word with something else, just click the Replace button in the Find dialog box to jump to the Replace dialog box explained in the following steps.

To replace a word or phrase with another word or phrase, perform the following steps:

1. Choose Edit, Replace, or press Ctrl+H. Or, from the Find dialog box, click the Replace button. The Replace dialog box appears, as shown in Figure 14.4.

FIGURE **14.4** The Replace dialog box.

2. In the Find What text box, type the word or phrase you want to search for.

3. In the Replace With text box, type the word or phrase you want to use as the replacement.

4. (Optional) Select either or both of the following options:

- Match Case finds text that matches the capitalization in the Find What text box.

- Find Whole Words Only skips any occurrences of the text that are a part of another word.

5. Click the Find Next button to find the first occurrence of the word.

6. If PowerPoint finds the text, click one of the following buttons:

- Replace replaces one occurrence of the Find What text with the Replace With text.

- Replace All replaces all occurrences of the Find What text (throughout your presentation) with the Replace With text.

- Find Next skips the current occurrence of the Find What text and moves to the next occurrence.

7. When PowerPoint has found and replaced all occurrences, a message appears to that effect. Click OK to close it. Or, if you are finished replacing text before PowerPoint comes to the last occurrence, click the Close button.

In this lesson, you learned how to check your presentation for misspelled words and typos, and how to find and replace words and phrases. In the next lesson, you learn how to draw lines and shapes on a slide.

LESSON 15

DRAWING LINES AND SHAPES

In this lesson, you learn how to use PowerPoint's drawing tools to draw graphic objects on a slide.

POWERPOINT'S DRAWING TOOLS

Although PowerPoint is not a drawing program per se, you can do some simple drawing with it. For example, you may want to draw a simple logo, or accent your slide with horizontal or vertical lines.

To this end, PowerPoint comes with several drawing tools to help you create lines and shapes. The Drawing toolbar displays these tools along the bottom of the presentation window in Slide and Notes Pages views.

There are two types of tools on the Drawing toolbar: tools for drawing lines and shapes, and tools for manipulating the graphic objects. Here's a look at the drawing ones:

TOOL	NAME	PURPOSE
	Line	Draws a straight line
	Arrow	Draws a straight line with an arrow on the end
	Rectangle	Draws a rectangle
	Ellipse	Draws an ellipse (oval)

DRAWING A LINE OR SHAPE

The general procedure for drawing an object is the same, no matter which object you draw:

1. Click the button on the Drawing toolbar for the line or shape you want to draw. For example, to draw a rectangle, click the Rectangle button.

2. Move the mouse pointer to where you want one end of the line or one corner of the object to be anchored.

3. Hold down the mouse button, and drag to where you want the opposite end of the line or corner of the object to appear. Figure 15.1 shows the procedure for drawing a rectangle.

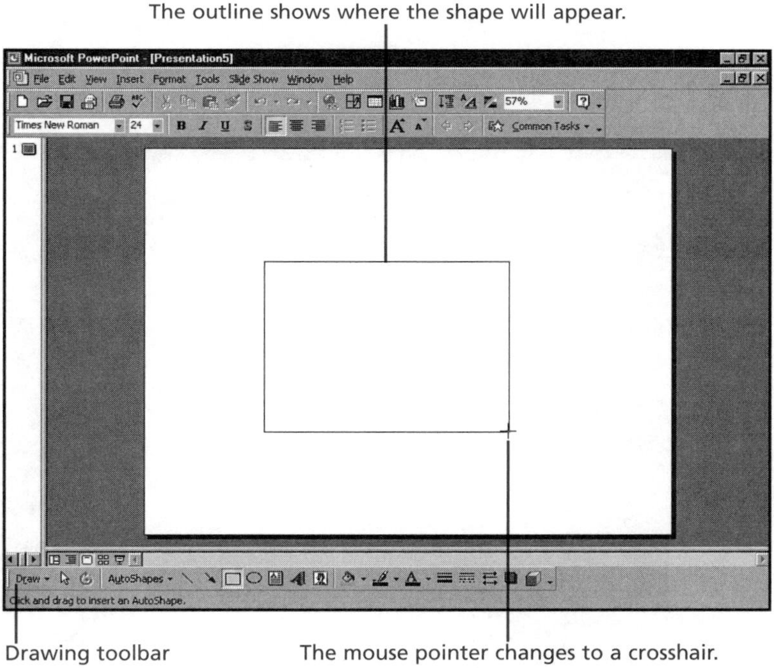

The outline shows where the shape will appear.

Drawing toolbar   The mouse pointer changes to a crosshair.

FIGURE 15.1 The Drawing toolbar contains tools for drawing lines and basic shapes.

4. Release the mouse button. The finished line or shape appears.

Squares and Circles You can draw a perfect square or circle by holding down the Shift key as you use the Rectangle or Ellipse tool, respectively.

WORKING WITH AUTOSHAPES

Drawing a complex shape with the rudimentary tools available to you can be frustrating. That's why PowerPoint comes with several predrawn objects, called AutoShapes, that you can use. To draw one of these objects, perform the following steps:

1. Click the AutoShapes button on the Drawing toolbar. A menu of shape types appears.

2. Click the type of shape you want. For example, if you want an arrow, choose Block Arrows. The AutoShapes palette appears for that type of shape, as shown in Figure 15.2.

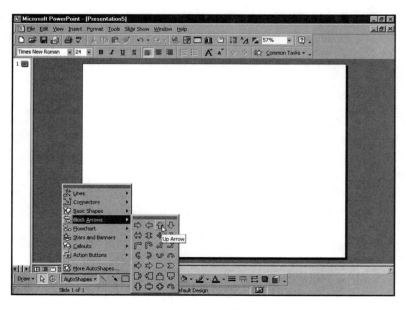

FIGURE **15.2** Select the shape you want from the AutoShapes palette.

3. Click the shape you want to draw.

4. Move the mouse pointer to where you want a corner or the center of the shape to be.

5. (Optional) While drawing the object, hold down one or both of the following keys: Ctrl to draw the shape out from a center point, or Shift to draw a shape that retains the dimensions shown on the AutoShapes palette.

6. Hold down the mouse button and drag the mouse to draw the object.

7. Release the mouse button. The shape appears, as shown in Figure 15.3.

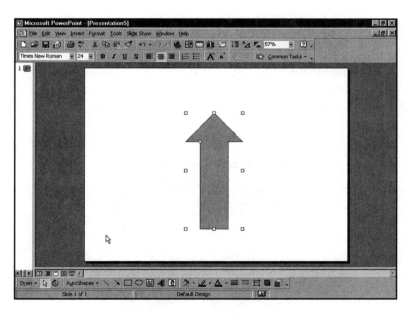

FIGURE 15.3 You can draw an AutoShape like this arrow as easily as any simple rectangle.

Changing an Existing Shape You can change an existing shape into a different shape. Select the shape you want to change, click the Draw button on the Drawing toolbar, select Change AutoShape, and click the shape you want to use.

ADDING TEXT TO A SHAPE

You can add text to any drawn shape. Unlike overlaying a shape with a text box, text typed into a shape stays with the shape when you move it. To insert text into your drawing, follow these steps:

1. Click the shape in which you want the text to appear.

2. Type the text. As you type, the text appears in a single line across the object.

3. (Optional) Select Format, AutoShape. The Format AutoShape dialog box appears.

4. Click the Text Box tab to display the options shown in Figure 15.4.

FIGURE **15.4** Use the Text Box tab to position your text inside the object.

5. Open the Text Anchor Point drop-down list and choose a position for the text in relation to the shape. (Middle is the default.)

6. Set margins for all four sides of the shape (Left, Right, Top, and Bottom), establishing how much white space will be left between the edges of the shape and the text.

7. (Optional) Select any of the following check boxes:

   • Word Wrap Text in AutoShape   Wraps text to another line if the text is wider than the shape.

   • Resize AuthoShape to Fit Text   Makes the shape larger or smaller so the text fits exactly within the margins you specify in step 5.

   • Rotate Text Within AutoShape by 90°   Rotates the text to run the other way (usually vertically) to help it fit better in the shape.

 Viewing the Effects of Your Changes   You can drag the title bar of the dialog box to move the dialog box away from the object. Then you can view the effects of your changes by clicking the Preview button before you click OK to save your changes.

8. Click OK to save your changes.

You can change the style and alignment of the text in an object in the same way you can change style and alignment in any text box. Refer to Lessons 11, 12, and 13 for details.

TIPS FOR WORKING WITH OBJECTS

Here are some quick tips that can save you some time and reduce frustration as you begin working with objects. You learn more about manipulating objects in Lessons 19, "Positioning and Sizing Objects," and 20, "Formatting Objects."

- If you're going to use the same tool to draw several objects in a row, double-click the tool. The tool stays selected and you don't have to reclick it after you draw each shape.

- To draw an object out from the center rather than from a corner, hold down the Ctrl key while dragging.

- To select an object, click it.

- To delete an object, select it and press Delete.

- To move an object, select it and drag one of its lines.

- To resize or reshape an object, select it and drag one of its handles.

- To copy an object, hold down the Ctrl key while dragging it.

In this lesson, you learned how to use PowerPoint's drawing tools to add drawings to your slides. In the next lesson, you learn how to add clip art and other pictures to a slide.

LESSON 16
ADDING CLIP ART AND OTHER IMAGES

In this lesson, you learn how to add PowerPoint clip art to your presentations, as well as images from other sources.

INTRODUCING THE CLIP GALLERY

One of the major changes between Office 2000 and the previous version is the improved Clip Gallery. The Clip Gallery, shown in Figure 16.1, manages artwork, sounds, and videos ("motion clips"). In this lesson, you learn to use it for artwork; in the following lesson, we revisit it for sounds and videos.

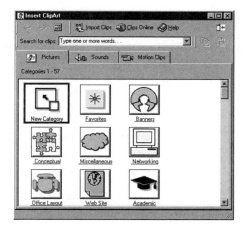

FIGURE 16.1 The Clip Gallery manages pictures, motion clips, and sounds, all in one convenient place.

Clip Art A collection of previously created images or pictures that you can place on a slide. Microsoft PowerPoint comes with clip art, and you can buy more from other sources too.

You can open the Clip Gallery in any of these ways:

- Click the Clip Art button on the Drawing toolbar.
- Select Insert, Picture, Clip Art.
- Select Insert, Movies and Sounds, Sound from Gallery.
- Select Insert, Movies and Sounds, Movie from Gallery.

All of these methods open the Clip Gallery, but a different tab appears on top depending on which method you used. For example, if you use Insert, Picture, Clip Art, the Pictures tab appears on top, as shown in Figure 16.1. Sometimes the dialog box title is different; for example, in Figure 16.1, it's Insert ClipArt. But it's the same old Clip Gallery any way you get there.

 PowerPoint on the Web Click the Clips Online button in the Clip Gallery dialog box (shown in Figure 16.1) to connect to Microsoft's Web site and download additional clip art.

INSERTING CLIP ART ON A SLIDE

To insert a piece of the clip art that comes with PowerPoint, follow these steps:

1. Open the Clip Gallery (Insert, Picture, Clip Art).
2. Click the category that represents the type of clip you want.
3. Click the clip you want to use. A pop-up menu of buttons appears.

4. Click the first button on the list, which is Insert Clip. See Figure 16.2.

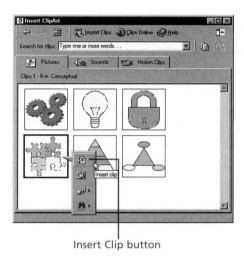

Insert Clip button

FIGURE **16.2**   The Clip Gallery manages pictures, clip art, videos, and sounds, all in one convenient place.

5. Close the Clip Gallery window. Your clip appears on the slide.

6. Resize and reposition the clip as needed. Refer to Lesson 19, "Positioning and Sizing Objects," for help.

 File Size Alert   Artwork, movies, and sounds can really add a lot to a PowerPoint presentation on the Web, but they also add to the size of the file, and consequently, to the time it will take a reader to download it. For this reason, try to be judicious in your use of media on presentations designed for Web use.

ADDING ART TO THE CLIP GALLERY

You can place most types of images in the Clip Gallery for easy reference, even those that did not come with PowerPoint. To add some art to the Clip Gallery, follow these steps:

1. In the Clip Gallery, click the Import Clips button.

2. In the Add Clip to Clip Gallery dialog box, locate and select the file you want to add. See Figure 16.3.

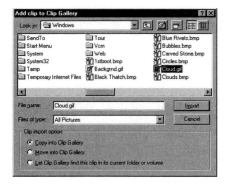

FIGURE 16.3 Choose the artwork that you want to be able to access through the Clip Gallery.

3. Choose one of the following option buttons:

   Copy into Clip Gallery   Choose this to make a copy of the graphic and place it in the same folder as the clip art images that come with PowerPoint. This is a good choice if the clip's original location is not always available (for example, on a network or a CD-ROM).

   Move into Clip Gallery   Choose this to move the graphic into the clip art folder.

   Let Clip Gallery find this clip in its current folder or volume Choose this to create a shortcut to the file's original location in the Clip Gallery. This is usually the best choice, as it saves disk space.

4. Click Import to import the clip. The Clip Properties dialog box appears.

5. Type a description in the Description of This Clip field on the Description tab.

6. Click the Categories tab, and place a check mark next to each category to which you want to assign the clip (see Figure 16.4). You should assign it to at least one category. Create a new category if needed by clicking the New Category button.

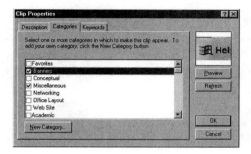

FIGURE **16.4** Categorize the graphic so it will appear in some of your Clip Gallery categories.

7. (Optional) Click the Keywords tab. Then click the New Keyword button and enter a keyword that describes the clip. Click OK to accept that keyword. Repeat to add as many keywords as you like. You will be able to use these keywords later when searching for clips.

8. Click OK. The clip is added to the Clip Gallery.

INSERTING A GRAPHIC FROM A FILE

If you have an image stored on disk, you can quickly place it on a slide without using with the Clip Gallery. You might want to do this, rather than adding the image to the Clip Gallery, if you are going to use the image only sporadically and don't need to keep it on file.

To place a graphic image from disk on a slide:

1. Select the slide on which the image should be placed.

2. Select Insert, Picture, From File. The Insert Picture dialog box appears (see Figure 16.5).

View button

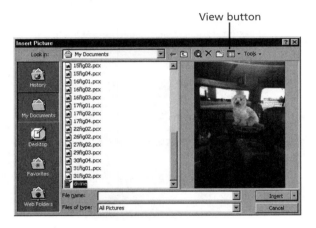

FIGURE 16.5   Use the Insert Picture dialog box to place any graphics image on a slide.

3. Select the picture you want to use. You can see a preview of the pictures in the Preview pane to the left of the file list. If the preview does not appear, click the View button (shown in Figure 16.5) until it comes into view.

4. Click Insert to place the image on the slide.

If the picture is too big or too small, you can drag the selection handles (the small squares) around the edge of the image to resize it. (Hold down Shift to proportionally resize.) Refer to Lesson 19 for more details about resizing and cropping.

Link It Up You can link a graphic to the presentation, so that whenever the original changes, the version in the presentation changes too. Just open the drop-down list on the Insert button in the Insert Picture dialog box (Figure 16.5) and choose Link to File. You learn about object linking and embedding in Lesson 18, "Object Linking and Embedding."

In this lesson, you learned how to add clip art and other images to your slides. In the next lesson, you learn how to add sounds and videos and control when they play.

LESSON 17

ADDING SOUNDS AND MOVIES

In this lesson, you learn how to add sound and video clips to a PowerPoint presentation.

FOUR WAYS TO INCLUDE SOUNDS IN A PRESENTATION

You can use sounds in any of these ways:

- You can insert a sound clip as an icon on a slide. When you click the icon, the sound plays. You can do this either from the Clip Gallery or from a file, just as you did with artwork in Lesson 16, "Adding Clip Art and Other Images."

- You can assign a sound to another object on a slide, so that when you click the object, the sound plays.

- You can assign a sound to an animated object on the slide, so that when the object appears, the sound plays.

- You can assign a sound to a transition between two slides, so that when the new slide appears, the sound plays.

In this lesson, we look at the first two methods, which both involve placing a sound clip directly on the slide. You learn about animation and transitions in Lesson 22, "Transitions and Animation."

PLACING A SOUND ON A SLIDE

To insert a sound clip as an object on a slide, you can either use the Clip Gallery or insert it from a file. The Clip Gallery may not have a very good selection of sound files unless you specifically import some, so you might have better luck with the "from file" method.

To insert a sound clip from a file:

1. Choose Insert, Movies and Sounds, Sound from File.

2. In the Insert Sound dialog box, navigate to the drive and folder containing the sound you want to use. See Figure 17.1.

FIGURE 17.1 Choose the sound clip you want to include on your slide.

3. Select the sound clip, and then click OK.

 Sample Sounds If you need some sounds to practice with, try the Windows\Media folder on your hard disk.

To place a sound from the Clip Gallery, use these steps instead:

1. Choose Insert, Movies and Sounds, Sound from Gallery).

2. Click the Sounds tab to display the available sounds. If there aren't any, you'll need to import some with the Import Clips button before you can continue. Refer to Lesson 16 for help.

3. Click the clip you want to use. A pop-up menu of buttons appears.

4. Click the first button on the list, which is Insert Clip.

5. Close the Clip Gallery window. Your sound clip's icon appears on the slide. It looks like a little speaker.

6. Resize and reposition the sound icon on the slide as needed. Refer to Lesson 19, "Positioning and Sizing Objects" for help.

ASSOCIATING A SOUND WITH ANOTHER OBJECT ON THE SLIDE

If you want to avoid having a sound icon on your slide, you can associate the sound with some other object on the slide already, such as a graphic. To do so, follow these steps:

1. Right-click the object to which you want to assign the sound.

2. Choose Action Settings from the shortcut menu.

3. If you want the sound to play when the object is pointed at, click the Mouse Over tab. Otherwise, click the Mouse Click tab.

4. Mark the Play Sound check box. A drop-down list of sounds becomes available. See Figure 17.2.

5. Open the Play Sound drop-down list and choose the sound you want.

   If the sound you want is not on the list, choose Other Sound and locate the sound using the Add Sound dialog box that appears. Select the sound from there and click OK.

6. When you have chosen the sound you want, click OK to close the Action Settings dialog box.

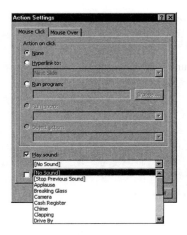

FIGURE 17.2   Choose a sound to be associated with the object.

Now when you are giving the presentation, you can play the sound by clicking on (or pointing at) the object. To test this, jump to Slide Show view (View, Slide Show) and try it out. Press Esc to return to PowerPoint when finished testing.

PLACING A MOVIE ON A SLIDE

The procedures for placing a movie on a slide are very much the same as those for a sound. You can place a movie using the Clip Gallery (Insert, Movies and Sounds, Movie from Gallery) or from a file (Insert, Movies and Sounds, Movie from File). Refer to "Placing a Sound on a Slide," earlier in this lesson, and substitute "movie" for "sound" in all steps.

There is one small difference when you're inserting a movie: PowerPoint may ask you whether you want the movie to play automatically in the slide show. If you see this dialog box, click Yes or No.

CHOOSING WHEN MOVIES AND SOUNDS SHOULD PLAY

Slides are static, for the most part. They appear and then they sit there. Movies and sounds, on the other hand, are dynamic—they play at certain times.

The default when you place a movie or sound on a slide is that the object does not activate until you click it. A slide may contain, for example, a recorded narration that explains a particular graph on the slide, but the narration will not play until the person giving the presentation clicks the sound icon to activate it.

When a Movie Isn't a Movie Most of the "motion clips" you get with PowerPoint, or that you download from the Microsoft Web site, are not true movie clips, but rather animated graphic files in the GIF format. These are not the same type of file as the .AVI or .MOV files that you create with real animation programs. PowerPoint sees them as graphics rather than as movies, and does not allow you to change their play settings. If the steps that follow do not work for your video clip, it may be an animated GIF rather than a real movie.

However, you may want some sounds or movies to play automatically at certain times in the presentation. You can specify this if prompted when you initially place the clip on the slide, as mentioned in the preceding section. Or, you can change the setting later with the following procedure:

1. Click the object (the sound icon or movie image) on the slide.

2. Select Slide Show, Custom Animation. The Custom Animation dialog box appears (see Figure 17.3).

3. Click the Order & Timing tab.

4. In the Start Animation section, choose On Mouse Click or Automatically—your choice.

5. If you choose Automatically, enter the number of seconds that PowerPoint should pause after the previous event before playing the object.

6. Click OK.

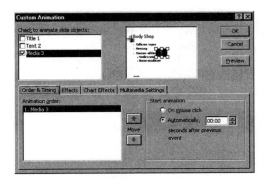

FIGURE 17.3   Use this dialog box to set when and how a sound or movie plays.

 Previous Event?   If this is the only media clip on this slide, the previous event is the slide itself being displayed. If there is more than one media clip on the slide, you can control which order they activate in by switching around their order in the Animation order list shown in Figure 17.3.

7. Switch to Slide Show view to test the slide, making sure you have set up the sound or animation to play when you want it to.

 Continuous Play   You can set a sound or animation to loop continuously by clicking the Multimedia Settings tab in the Custom Animation dialog box, and then the More Options button. Select both the Loop Until Stopped and Rewind Movie When Done Playing check boxes.

In this chapter, you learned how to place sounds and movies in your presentation for great multimedia effects. In the next chapter, you learn how to include content from other programs in your PowerPoint presentation.

LESSON 18
OBJECT LINKING AND EMBEDDING

In this lesson, you learn about Object Linking and Embedding (OLE), and you find out how to link data from other programs to your PowerPoint presentation.

WHAT IS OLE?

Object linking and embedding, or OLE, is a way to ensure that your documents are always up-to-date. When you import or paste a graphic, chart, or other object into a presentation, the pasted piece is "dead"—that is, it does not automatically change when the original changes. In contrast, when you link an object to a presentation, the object stays "alive." When you open and edit it in its native program, PowerPoint reflects those changes in its copy of the object.

LINKING OR EMBEDDING: WHAT'S THE DIFFERENCE?

Linking and embedding are actually two distinct things, although few people really understand the difference.

Embedding is what happens whenever you insert an object into a presentation using the menu choices Insert, Object. PowerPoint places the object in the presentation, and you double-click it to open its native program and edit the object on the spot.

When you link a file from another program to your PowerPoint presentation, you can make changes to that file outside of PowerPoint, and the copy in the PowerPoint presentation updates automatically. How? When PowerPoint opens the presentation, it retrieves each linked object again, getting the freshest copy of the object.

LINKING A FILE TO A PRESENTATION

If you have a file in another program (for instance, a graphic in the Windows Paint program), you can link it to a PowerPoint presentation. To link the file to your presentation, follow these steps:

1. Display the slide onto which you want to place the object.

2. Choose Insert, Object. The Insert Object dialog box appears.

3. Click Create from File. The dialog box changes, as shown in Figure 18.1.

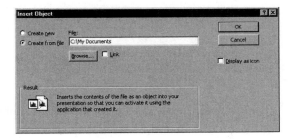

FIGURE 18.1   The Insert Object dialog box enables you to link an object.

4. Type the complete path and filename of the file you want to link, or click the Browse button to use a dialog box to find it.

5. Select the Link check box. This is important! It makes the difference between linking *and* embedding and merely embedding.

6. Click OK.

EMBEDDING AN OBJECT IN A PRESENTATION

With linking, a file has to already exist. You can't create a file on the spot and then link it.

With embedding, you have this added flexibility. You can either embed an existing file, or create and embed a new one by opening the native program right there in PowerPoint.

To embed an existing file, just follow the steps for linking in the preceding section, but do not select the Link check box. To create a new file and embed it, perform the following steps:

1. Display the slide onto which you want to place the object.

2. Choose Insert, Object. The Insert Object dialog box appears.

3. Click Create New. You see the options shown in Figure 18.2.

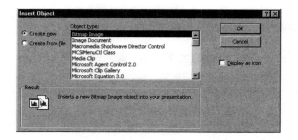

FIGURE 18.2   Use these options to create a new file and embed it.

4. Choose an object type, based on the program you are using to create the object. For instance, you can choose Bitmap Image to embed a graphics file.

5. Click OK. A small box in the center of the slide opens, and the controls for that program appear. You create your new object in that box (see Figure 18.3).

6. Create the new file using the program. (Refer to the program's documentation for instructions on how to use that program.)

7. Click anywhere outside the box to return to your PowerPoint presentation. The box remains on the slide, and you can move the box around like any other object.

8. If you want to edit the object, just double-click it.

In this lesson, you learned to link and embed objects in your presentation. In the next lesson, you learn about repositioning and resizing objects on a slide.

The toolbar is from Paint.

These are Paint menus.   Here is my PowerPoint slide.

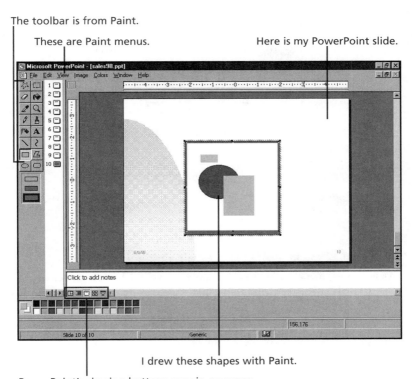

I drew these shapes with Paint.

PowerPoint's viewing buttons remain onscreen.

FIGURE 18.3   You can create a graphic to embed in your PowerPoint slide.

LESSON 19

POSITIONING AND SIZING OBJECTS

In this lesson, you learn how to select, copy, move, rotate, and resize objects on a slide.

SELECTING OBJECTS

As you may have already discovered, objects are the building blocks you use to create slides in PowerPoint. Objects are the shapes you draw, the graphs you create, the pictures you import, and the text you type. In this and the next lesson, you will learn how to manipulate objects on your slides to create impressive presentations.

Before you can copy, move, rotate, or resize an object, you must first select the object. Change to Normal or Slide view, and perform one of the following steps to choose one or more objects:

- To select a single object, click it. (If you click text, a frame appears around the text. Click the frame to select the text object.)

- To select more than one object, hold down the Shift key while clicking on each object. Handles appear around the selected objects, as shown in Figure 20.1.

- To deselect selected objects, click anywhere outside the selected objects.

Selected text box   Selection handles

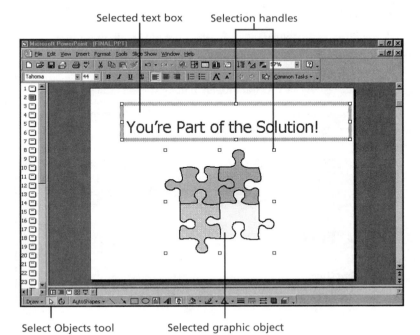

Select Objects tool   Selected graphic object

FIGURE 20.1 Handles indicate that objects are selected.

Using the Select Objects Tool The Select Objects tool on the Drawing toolbar (the button with the mouse pointer on it), enables you to quickly select a group of objects. Click the Select Objects tool and use the mouse pointer to drag a selection box around the objects you want to select. When you release the mouse button, PowerPoint selects the objects inside the box.

WORKING WITH LAYERS OF OBJECTS

As you place objects onscreen, they may start to overlap, making it difficult or impossible to select the objects in the lower layers. To move objects in layers, perform the following steps:

1. Click the object you want to move up or down in the stack.

2. Click the Draw button on the Drawing toolbar to open the Draw menu, and select Order, as shown in Figure 20.2.

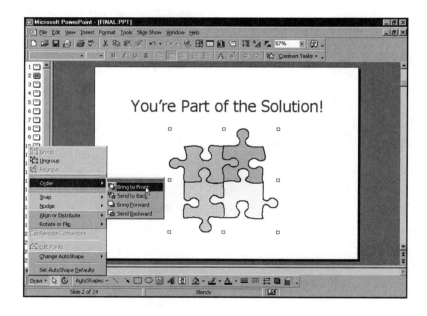

You're Part of the Solution!

FIGURE 20.2 Use the Draw menu on the Drawing toolbar to change the layer on which a graphic appears on your slide.

3. Select one of the following options:

   • Bring to Front brings the object to the top of the stack.

   • Send to Back sends the object to the bottom of the stack.

   • Bring Forward brings the object up one layer.

   • Send Backward sends the object back one layer.

GROUPING AND UNGROUPING OBJECTS

Each object you draw acts as an individual object. However, sometimes you want two or more objects to act as a group. For example, you may want to make the lines of several objects the same thickness, or group several objects together. If you want to treat two or more objects as a group, perform the following steps:

1. Select the objects you want to group. Remember, to select more than one object, hold down the Shift key as you click each one.

2. Click the Draw button on the Drawing toolbar to open the Draw menu, and then select Group.

3. To ungroup the objects, select any object in the group, and select Draw, Ungroup.

CUTTING, COPYING, AND PASTING OBJECTS

You can cut, copy, and paste objects on a slide to rearrange the objects or to use the objects to create a picture. When you cut an object, PowerPoint removes the object from the slide and places it in a temporary holding area called the Windows Clipboard. When you copy an object, the original object remains on the slide, and PowerPoint places a copy of it on the Clipboard. In either case, you can then paste the object from the Clipboard onto the current slide or another slide. To cut or copy an object, perform the following steps:

1. Select the object(s) you want to cut, copy, or move.

2. Right-click the selection and choose Cut or Copy from the short-cut menu. Or, select Edit, Cut or Edit, Copy, or click the Cut or Copy buttons on the Standard toolbar.

3. Display the slide on which you want to place the cut or copied object(s). (You can also open a different Windows program to paste it into if you prefer.)

4. Select Edit, Paste, or click the Paste button on the Standard toolbar. PowerPoint pastes the object(s) on the slide.

Keyboard Shortcuts You can press Ctrl+X to cut,
Ctrl+C to copy, and Ctrl+V to paste instead of using
the toolbar buttons or the menu.

5. Move the mouse pointer over any of the pasted objects, hold
down the mouse button, and drag the objects to where you want
them.

6. Release the mouse button.

Deleting an Object To remove an object without
placing it on the Clipboard, select the object and then
press the Delete key, or select Edit, Clear.

Dragging and Dropping Objects The quickest way to
copy or move objects is to drag and drop them. Select
the objects you want to move, position the mouse
pointer over any of the selected objects, hold down
the mouse button, and drag the objects where you
want them. To copy the objects, hold down the Ctrl
key while dragging.

ROTATING AN OBJECT

The Rotate tools enable you to revolve an object around a center point.
Not all pictures can be rotated; for example, bitmap images can't. If the
selected picture can't be rotated, the Free Rotate tool will not be available.

To rotate an object to your own specifications, using Free Rotate, do the following:

1. Click the object you want to rotate.

2. Click the Free Rotate tool on the Drawing toolbar. The selection handles on the centering line change to circles.

3. Hold down the mouse button and drag the circular handle until the object is in the position you want. (See Figure 20.3.)

Dotted outline shows new position

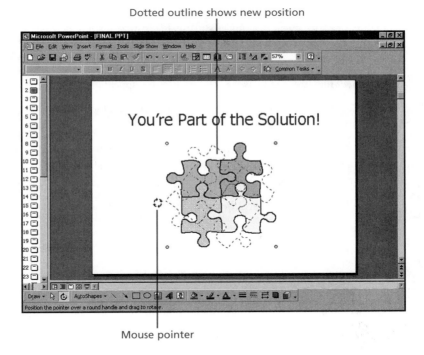

Mouse pointer

FIGURE 20.3 You can drag the circular selection handle to rotate the object.

4. Release the mouse button.

Other Rotate Options   The Draw menu (on the Drawing toolbar; refer to Figure 20.2) contains a Rotate or Flip submenu that provides additional options for rotating objects. You can flip an object 90 degrees left or right, or flip the object over on the centering line to create a mirrored image of it.

RESIZING OBJECTS

There may be times when an object you create or import is not the right size for your slide presentation. You can resize the object by performing these steps:

1. Select the object to resize. Selection handles appear.

2. Drag one of the handles (the squares that surround the object) until the object is the desired size:

    - Drag a corner handle to change both the height and width of an object. PowerPoint retains the object's relative dimensions.

    - Drag a side, top, or bottom handle to change the height or width alone.

    - Hold down the Ctrl key while dragging to resize from the center of the picture.

3. Release the mouse button, and PowerPoint resizes the object (see Figure 20.4).

Dotted outline shows how big it will be

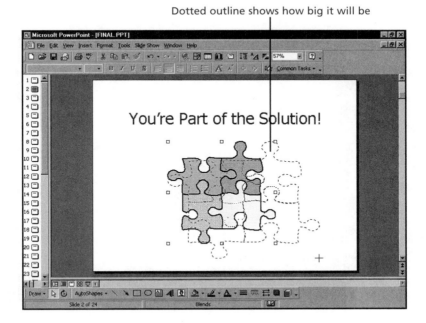

FIGURE 20.4   Drag a handle to resize an object.

CROPPING A PICTURE

Besides resizing a picture, you can crop it. That is, you can trim a side or corner of the picture to remove an element from the picture or cut off some white space. Only true pictures can be cropped; AutoShapes can't.

To crop a picture, perform the following steps:

1. Click the picture you want to crop.

2. If the Picture toolbar isn't shown, right-click the picture and select Show Picture Toolbar from the menu.

3. Click the Crop button on the Picture toolbar. The mouse pointer turns into a cropping tool. (See Figure 20.5.)

Mouse pointer ready to crop

Picture toolbar   Crop button

FIGURE 20.5   Use the cropping tool to chop off a section of the picture.

4. Move the mouse pointer over one of the handles. (Use a corner handle to crop two sides at once. Use a side, top, or bottom handle to crop only one side.)

5. Hold down the mouse button, and drag the pointer until the crop lines are where you want them.

6. Release the mouse button. The cropped section disappears.

7. Resize or move the picture as needed for its new placement.

In this lesson, you learned how to select, copy, move, rotate, and resize an object on a slide. In the next lesson, you learn how to change the lines and colors of an object.

LESSON 20
FORMATTING OBJECTS

In this lesson, you learn how to add borders, colors, patterns, shadows, and 3D effects to objects.

CHANGING LINE THICKNESS AND COLOR

In Lesson 16, "Drawing Lines and Shapes," you learned to draw your own artwork on a slide, and in Lesson 17, "Adding Clip Art and Other Images," you learned to import clip art and other graphics. You can change the appearance of both kinds of artwork by modifying the colors and lines, but the procedures are different depending on whether the art is predrawn (a file you have imported) or drawn by you with the PowerPoint drawing tools.

 Drawing versus Picture In PowerPoint terms, a drawing is artwork that you have created yourself using PowerPoint's drawing tools, while a picture is artwork that you have imported in (such as clip art). If you want to change an imported picture's colors, see the section "Changing the Colors of a Picture," later in this lesson.

CHANGING A DRAWING'S COLORS AND LINES

If the line or shape you draw is not the color you expect it to be, you can change it. With lines, you have only one color option: change the line. With shapes, you can change the color of both the inside (fill) and the outside border (line).

Follow these steps to change the lines or color of any object you've drawn:

1. Right-click the drawn object. A shortcut menu appears.

2. From the shortcut menu, select Format AutoShape, and then click the Colors and Lines tab (see Figure 21.1).

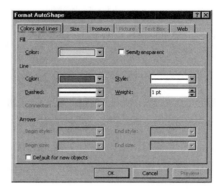

FIGURE 21.1   Use the Colors and Lines tab of the Format AutoShape dialog box to change the lines and colors for a drawn object.

 I Don't See Format AutoShape on the Menu! If you right-click a piece of clip art or other imported graphic, rather than one you've drawn yourself, you won't find the Format AutoShape command. However, you can select Format Picture instead and modify the picture's properties as explained in "Changing the Colors of a Picture," later in this lesson.

3. In the Fill section, open the Color list and select a different color for the inside of the shape. (This isn't applicable if the drawn object you're formatting is a line.) For more color choices, choose More Colors and select from the dialog box that appears.

4. In the Line section, open the Color drop-down list and choose a line color. For shapes, the Line setting affects the color of the shape's outside border.

Textures and Patterns From the Fill Color button's drop-down list, you can select Fill Effects. This opens a dialog box from which you can choose textures, patterns, and gradients. Some textures are really cool—they look like wood, marble, or granite.

Semitransparent? If you want to partially see through a shape to whatever is behind it, click the Semitransparent check box. For example, if you have a blue shape on a red background and you make the blue shape semitransparent, it appears to be made up equally of red and blue. If you put the same shape on a white background, the shape appears light blue, a mixture of blue and white.

5. Choose a line style from the Style drop-down list. You can choose thick or thin lines, double lines, and so on.

6. If you want a different thickness, change the number in the Weight text box to a higher or lower number. (Measurements are in points. A point is 1/72 of an inch.)

7. If you want the line to be dashed (broken), choose a dash style from the Dashed drop-down list.

8. If you want arrows at one or both ends of a line, choose the beginning and ending arrow styles from the Arrows drop-down list. (These controls will be unavailable if you are formatting a shape rather than a line.)

9. If you want to draw all objects with these colors and line styles, you can specify them as the default by clicking the Default for New Objects check box.

10. Click OK. PowerPoint applies your changes to the shape.

Changing the Entire Color Scheme If you want to change the entire color scheme for the presentation, don't mess around with individual objects—turn back to Lesson 9, "Working with Presentation Colors and Backgrounds," for instructions.

CHANGING THE COLORS OF A PICTURE

When you paste a clip art image or insert a picture on a slide, the picture appears in its original colors. These colors may clash with the colors in your presentation. To change the colors in a picture, perform the following steps:

1. Click the picture you want to change. A selection box appears around the picture.

2. Do either of the following to open the Recolor Picture dialog box shown in Figure 21.2:

   - If the Picture toolbar is not displayed, right-click the picture and select Show Picture Toolbar. Then click the Recolor Picture button on that toolbar.

   - Select Format, Colors and Lines. The Format Picture dialog box appears. Click the Picture tab, and then the Recolor button.

3. In the Change area, select Colors to change line colors, or Fills to change colors between the lines.

 Fills Isn't an Option! With some picture types, Fills will be unavailable to select. That's okay—go ahead and select the colors, and the filled-in areas in the picture should change just fine.

4. Select a color you want to change in the Original list. A check mark appears in the check box next to the color.

Use the scrollbar to see more colors

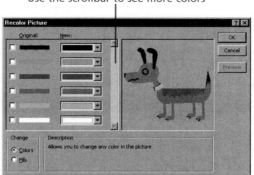

FIGURE 21.2   Use the Recolor Picture dialog box to change the colors in a picture.

5. Use the New drop-down menu to the right of the selected color to choose the color you want.

Using the More Colors Option   At the bottom of each color's drop-down menu is the More Colors option. Select this option if you want to use a color that is not listed on the menu.

6. Repeat steps 3 through 5 for each color you want to change.

7. If you want to revert to an original color, remove the check mark from beside it.

8. If the change does not show in the Preview pane of the dialog box, click the Preview button, and then drag the dialog box to the side to see a preview of the changes.

9. If the changes are okay, click OK to close the dialog box.

DRAWING A BORDER AROUND A PICTURE

You can frame any object (a picture, a text box, or whatever) by drawing a border around the object. (This is the same as changing the line style and thickness on a drawn object.)

To add a border to an object, perform the following steps in Slide view:

1. Select the object you want to frame with a border, such as a text box or clip art object.

2. Choose Format, Colors and Lines. A dialog box appears that's appropriate for the type of object you selected (for instance, Format Text Box for a text box) with the Colors and Lines tab on top, as shown in Figure 21.1.

3. Open the Color drop-down list and choose a color for the line.

4. Open the Style drop-down list and choose a thickness and style for the line.

5. If you want the line to be dotted or dashed, open the Dashed drop-down list and choose a dash style.

6. Click OK. The border appears around the object.

ADDING A SHADOW OR A 3D EFFECT

A shadow gives some depth to an object. Applying a 3D effect to an object does much the same thing, as you can see in Figure 21.3. The main difference is that a shadow just adds shading behind a two-dimensional object, while a 3D effect attempts to make the object appear fully three dimensional. Shadows work with all objects, but 3D effects work only with drawn artwork.

Original shape   Shape with 3D effect applied

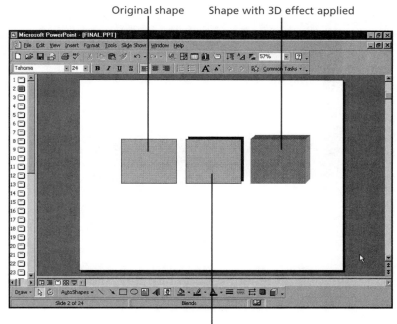

Shape with shadow applied

FIGURE 21.3 Shadows and 3D effects can keep your artwork from looking flat and boring.

ADDING A SHADOW

To add a shadow to an object, perform these steps:

1. Select the object to which you want to add a shadow.

2. Click the Shadow tool on the Drawing toolbar. A menu of shadow options appears (see Figure 21.4).

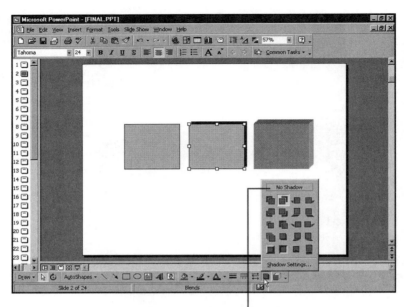

Click here to remove the shadow from an object.

FIGURE 21.4   Click the type of shadow you want to use.

3. Click the type of shadow you want. The shadow is applied to the object.

4. (Optional) To make fine adjustments to the shadow, click the Shadow tool again and select Shadow Settings, then use the Shadow toolbar that appears:

	Shadow On/Off	Toggles the shadow on/off
	Nudge Shadow Up	Extends the shadow slightly to the top
	Nudge Shadow Down	Extends the shadow slightly to the bottom
	Nudge Shadow Left	Extends the shadow slightly to the left

	Nudge Shadow Right	Extends the shadow slightly to the right
	Shadow Color	Changes the shadow color

ADDING A 3D EFFECT

Follow these steps to apply a 3D effect to an object:

1. Select the object. It must be an object you've drawn with the Drawing toolbar tools, not an imported piece of clip art.

2. Click the 3D button on the Drawing toolbar. The 3D tools appear (see Figure 21.5).

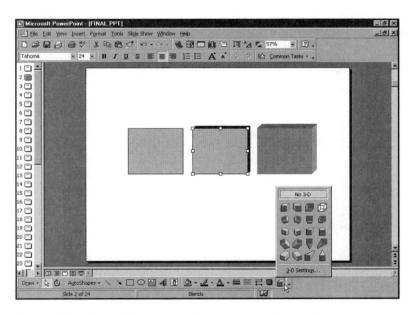

FIGURE 21.5 These 3D tools enable you to apply a variety of special 3D effects to a drawn object.

3. Click the 3D effect that you want.

4. (Optional) Click the 3D button again, and choose 3D Settings, then use the 3D toolbar that appears:

	Toggles between 3D and regular (2D)
	Tilts down
	Tilts up
	Tilts left
	Tilts right
	Adjusts depth
	Adjusts direction
	Adjusts lighting
	Changes surface
	Changes color

COPYING THE LOOK OF ANOTHER OBJECT

If your presentation contains an object that has the frame, fill, and shadow you want to use for another object, you can pick up those design elements and apply them to another object. To do this, perform the following steps:

1. Click the object with the style you want to copy.

2. Click the Format Painter button on the Standard toolbar. PowerPoint copies the style.

3. Click the object to which you want to apply the style. PowerPoint applies the copied style to the new object.

In this lesson, you learned how to use borders, colors, shadows, and 3D effects to change the look of individual objects on a slide. You also learned how to copy design elements from object to object. In the next lesson, you learn how to add a graph to a slide with Microsoft Graph.

LESSON 21

ADDING A GRAPH TO A SLIDE

Graphs are useful for illustrating trends and presenting numeric data in a format that others can understand. In this lesson, you learn how to create a graph and place it on a presentation slide.

INSERTING A GRAPH

PowerPoint comes with a program called Microsoft Graph that transforms raw data into professional-looking graphs. To create a graph, perform the following steps:

1. Display the slide to which you want to add the graph.

2. Click the Insert Chart button on the Standard toolbar, or select Insert, Chart. The Microsoft Graph window appears. In Figure 21.1, the Datasheet window is on top.

 Datasheet The datasheet is set up like a spreadsheet with rows, columns, and cells. Each rectangle in the datasheet is a cell that can hold text or numbers. Microsoft Graph converts the data you enter in the datasheet into a graph it displays in the Graph window.

---

3. First, you change the datasheet values to your own figures. Click inside the cell that contains a label or value you want to change, and type your entry.

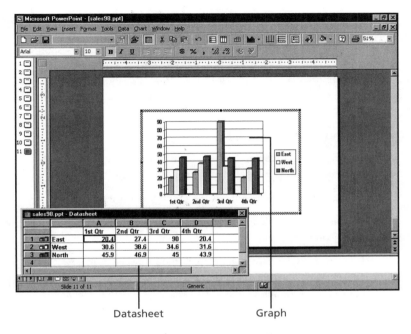

Datasheet   Graph

FIGURE 21.1 The Datasheet window appears in the front.

4. Click the next cell you want to change, or use the arrow keys to move from cell to cell.

5. Repeat steps 3 and 4 until you enter all your data.

6. Click the graph. The graph displays your datasheet data.

7. To leave Microsoft Graph and return to your slide in PowerPoint, click anywhere outside the graph.

 Redisplaying the Datasheet If you need to make a change in the datasheet after you create it, see the next section, "Editing the Datasheet."

Moving and Resizing the Graph   If the graph is too big or is in a bad location on the slide, you can resize and move it. Refer to Lesson 19, "Positioning and Sizing Objects," for details.

EDITING THE DATASHEET

If you return to your slide and later decide that you want to edit the data that your graph is based on, perform the following steps:

1. Display the slide that contains the graph you want to edit.

2. Double-click anywhere inside the graph. PowerPoint starts Microsoft Graph and displays the graph.

 3. If Microsoft Graph does not display the Datasheet window, choose View, Datasheet or click the View Datasheet button in the Microsoft Graph toolbar. The Datasheet window appears.

4. Use the Tab key to go to the cell that contains the value you want to change, and type your change.

5. When you are done, click anywhere inside the graph window.

In addition to editing individual data entries, you can cut, copy, and paste cells; delete and insert rows and columns; and adjust column widths. This list gives you a quick overview of how to edit your datasheet:

Selecting Cells   To select one cell, click it. To select several cells, drag the mouse pointer over the desired cells. To select a row or column, click the letter above the column or the number to the left of the row. To select all the cells, click the upper-left square in the datasheet.

Clearing Cells   To erase the contents of cells, select the cells, and select Edit, Clear. Select All (to clear contents and formatting), Contents (to remove only the contents), or Formats (to remove only the formatting). You can also press the Delete key to clear the contents (not the formatting), or right-click and choose Clear Contents.

Cutting or Copying Cells   To cut cells, select the cells you want to cut. Then select Edit, Cut, or click the Cut button. To copy cells, select the cells you want to copy. Then select Edit, Copy, or click the Copy button. You also can right-click and select Cut or Copy from the shortcut menu instead.

Pasting Cells   To paste copied or cut cells into a datasheet, select the cell in the upper-left corner of the area in which you want to paste the cut or copied cells. Select Edit, Paste, or click the Paste button. You also can right-click the destination area and select Paste from the shortcut menu.

Inserting Blank Cells   To insert blank cells into your datasheet, select the row, column, or number of cells you want to insert. (Rows will be inserted above the current row. Columns will be inserted to the left of the current column.) Select Insert, Cells. If you select a row or column, PowerPoint inserts the row or column. If you select one or more cells, the Insert Cells dialog box appears, asking whether you want to shift surrounding cells down or to the right. Select your preference, and click OK. As a shortcut, you can right-click where you want the cells to go and select Insert from the shortcut menu.

Changing the Column Width   If you type entries that are too wide for a particular column, you may want to adjust the column width. Move the mouse pointer over the column letter at the top of the column you want to change. Move the mouse pointer to the right until it turns into a double-headed arrow. Hold down the mouse button and drag the mouse until the column is the desired width.

CHANGING THE DATA SERIES

Say you create a graph that shows the sales figures for several salespersons over four quarters. You wanted each column in the graph to represent a salesperson, but instead, the columns represent quarters. To fix the graph, you can swap the data series by performing the following steps:

1. Open the Data menu.

2. Select Series in Rows or Series in Columns.

> 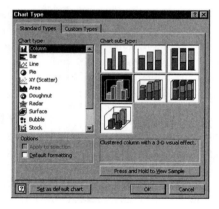 **Quick Data Series Swap** To quickly swap data series, click the By Row or By Column button on the Standard toolbar.

CHANGING THE CHART TYPE

By default, Microsoft Graph creates a three-dimensional column chart. If you want Microsoft Graph to display your data in a different type of chart, perform the following steps:

1. Choose Chart, Chart Type. The Chart Type dialog box appears, as shown in Figure 21.2.

FIGURE 21.2 Pick the chart type you want.

2. Click the desired chart type from the Chart Type area.

3. Click a subtype from the Chart Subtype area. The subtypes change depending on what type you chose in step 2.

4. (Optional) To view a sample before you accept the chart, click and hold down the mouse button on the Press and Hold to View Sample button.

5. (Optional) To make this type of chart the default, click the Set as Default Chart button.

6. Click OK.

 Quick Change To quickly change the chart type, click the Chart Type button on the toolbar and select from a drop-down list of chart types that appears.

 PowerPoint on the Web If you are designing a chart for Web viewing, keep it as simple and self-explanatory as possible, avoiding the more complicated chart types. Keep in mind that there will not be a narrator presenting the slide show who can explain what the chart means; the readers will need to be able to understand it on their own.

APPLYING CUSTOM CHART TYPES

Microsoft Graph comes with several predesigned chart formats that you can apply to your chart. You select the custom chart type you want, and Microsoft Graph reformats your chart, giving it a professional look. Here's how you use Custom Chart Types to select a chart design:

1. Choose Chart, Chart Type. The Chart Type dialog box appears, as shown in Figure 21.2.

2. Click the Custom Types tab. The display changes to the one shown in Figure 21.3.

3. From the Chart Type list, choose a chart type. In the Sample area, Microsoft Graph creates a sample of the selected chart type.

4. Click OK. Microsoft Graph reformats the chart using the selected custom type.

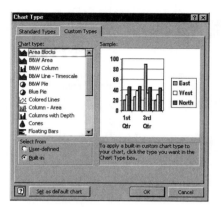

FIGURE 21.3   Select a custom chart type using the Custom Types tab.

In this lesson, you learned how to create and insert graphs on a slide, enter and edit graph data, and change graph types. In the next lesson, you learn how to set up transitions and animation effects.

LESSON 22

TRANSITIONS AND ANIMATION

In this lesson, you learn about transitions between slides and animation effects within slides.

SETTING UP TRANSITIONS

An onscreen slide show is a lot like the slide show you put on using a slide projector. However, with an onscreen slide show, you can add impressive and professional visual effects (transitions and effects) that provide smooth and attention-getting movements from one slide or object to the next.

 Transitions and Effects A *transition* is a way of moving from one slide to the next. For example, with a vertical blinds transition, the slide takes on the look of window blinds that turn to reveal the next slide. An *effect* is also an animated movement from one thing to another, but it pertains to individual objects on the slide, such as a bulleted list or a movie, rather than to the appearance or disappearance of the entire slide.

A transition, as explained previously, is an animation that moves the presentation along from one slide to the next. The default transition is for one slide to simply vanish and the next slide to appear in its place.

To apply a slide transition to a slide, perform the following steps:

1. Open the presentation to which you want to add transitions.

2. Switch to Slide Sorter view. The Slide Sorter toolbar appears at the top of the screen. (See Figure 22.1.)

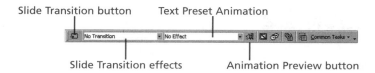

Slide Transition button   Text Preset Animation

Slide Transition effects   Animation Preview button

FIGURE 22.1   In Slide Sorter view, you have an extra toolbar to work with that controls transitions.

3. Select the slide to which you want to add a transition. To select more than one slide, hold down the Shift key as you select. To select all slides, press Ctrl+A.

4. Select Slide Show, Slide Transition, or click the Slide Transition button. The Slide Transition dialog box appears, as shown in Figure 22.2.

FIGURE 22.2   Use this dialog box to add transition effects and timing to the slides you select.

5. Open the Effect drop-down list and choose a transition effect. (Keep an eye on the preview area to see a demonstration of the effect.)

 Oops! I Missed It!   PowerPoint immediately demonstrates a transition on the picture in the dialog box when you select it. You can click the picture to see the demonstration again if you miss it the first time.

6. At the bottom of the Effect area, select the desired speed for the transition to take effect: Slow, Medium, or Fast.

7. To associate a sound with the transition, select one from the Sound drop-down list. (To loop the sound so that it plays over and over, select the Loop Until Next Sound check box.)

8. Click the Apply button to apply the settings to the slide(s) you selected, or click Apply to All to apply the settings to all slides in the presentation.

Quick Transition Setup   To quickly apply a transition (without timing), pull down the Transitions drop-down list on the Slide Sorter toolbar (see Figure 22.1) and select the desired transition.

ADDING ANIMATION EFFECTS

While transitions affect an entire slide, effects apply to individual elements on the slide. For instance, you might want the slide's background and title to appear first (using a transition), and then have the individual items on a bulleted list appear, one at a time, beneath the heading.

Animation   When most people think of animation, they think of cartoons, but PowerPoint uses "animation" to mean the movement onscreen that acts as a transition from one object or slide to the next.

ANIMATING THE TEXT ON A SLIDE

The simplest form of animation is to animate the text on a slide separately from its title and background. When you choose one of these effects, the title and background appear as specified by the transition, and then the rest of the slide's text appears, paragraph by paragraph, using the chosen effect.

To apply simple animation effects to an object on a slide, follow these steps:

1. In Slide Sorter view, select the slide that contains the text you want to animate.

2. Open the Text Preset Animation drop-down list on the Slide Sorter toolbar and select an animation effect for the text on that slide.

3. Switch to Slide Show view to preview the effect. The title and background of the slide appears.

4. Press the Page Down key or click the mouse button. The first paragraph (or bullet) appears using the chosen effect.

5. Keep pressing Page Down or clicking until all of the slide's text is onscreen.

6. Press Esc to return to Slide Sorter view.

  Animation Preview   You can also click the Animation Preview button on the Slide Sorter toolbar to preview the animation without switching to Slide Show view.

CUSTOM ANIMATION

If you want to get more detailed with an object's animation, or if you want to animate multimedia objects (like sounds and video on the slide), you must use custom animation. Here's how:

1. In Normal or Slide view, display the slide containing the object(s) to animate.

2. Select Slide Show, Custom Animation. The Custom Animation dialog box appears (see Figure 22.3).

3. In the Check to animate slide objects list, click to place a check mark next to the object you want to animate. The object appears in the Animation Order list.

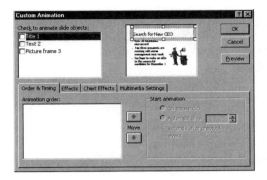

FIGURE 22.3   Use the Custom Animation dialog box to animate objects on a slide using precise settings.

4. On the Order & Timing tab, specify when the animation should take place:

   • Leave the On Mouse Click option button selected if you want the animation to happen when you click the mouse (that is, at your command).

   • Click the Automatically option button and specify a number of seconds that should elapse between the action before it and this animation.

5. Repeat steps 3 and 4 until all the objects you want to animate appear in the Animation Order list.

6. Use the up and down arrow buttons to rearrange the items on the Animation Order list if needed. The slide will "build" in the order you specify here.

7. Now it's time to choose the effect itself. Select the object in the Animation Order list for which you want to specify an effect.

8. Click the Effects tab. The Effects controls appear, as shown in Figure 22.4.

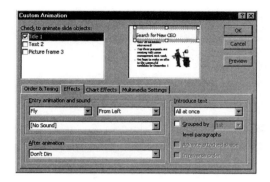

FIGURE 22.4   Use the Effects controls to specify what animation and sound will apply to a slide.

9. In the Entry Animation and Sound section, select an effect from the Entry Animation drop-down list (the top one).

10. (Optional) Select a sound to accompany the effect from the Sound drop-down list (the bottom one).

11. Select another animated object from the Check to animate slide objects box, and repeat steps 9 and 10 for it.

12. When you are done setting up effects, click OK.

13. Use Slide Show view or click the Preview button to test your work.

OTHER ANIMATION OPTIONS

As you saw in Figure 22.4, there are many more options in the Custom Animation dialog box for setting up your animation than can be covered here, including Chart Effects and Multimedia Effects. There simply isn't enough space to delve into them all in this book. Experiment with them, and find your favorite special effects. Here are some ideas to get you started:

*   In the Introduce text drop-down list, you can choose to have text appear word-by-word, or even letter-by-letter.

- If you have multiple levels of bullet points in your text, you can animate by a different level other than 1st by choosing it from the Grouped by drop-down list.

- You can build text from the bottom to the top by selecting the In Reverse Order check box.

- You can choose to dim the object after it has been animated. This might come in handy, for instance, if you have a bulleted list in which you want the point you are currently talking about "bright" and the other points "dim." To do so, choose an effect from the After Animation drop-down list.

- As you learned in Lesson 17, "Adding Sounds and Movies," you can control how a sound or video clip plays by clicking the Play Settings tab and setting options there. This tab's controls are unavailable unless the selected object is "playable" (in other words, some type of media clip).

In this lesson, you learned how to add timed transitions and animations to your slides. In the next lesson, you learn how to create speaker's notes pages.

LESSON 23

CREATING SPEAKER'S NOTES

In this lesson, you learn how to create speaker's notes to help you during the delivery of your presentation.

CREATING SPEAKER'S NOTES PAGES

The problem with many presentations is that the presenter merely flips from one slide to the next, without telling the audience the point or providing an overview that adds meaning. To make your slide show a success, you can put together a set of speaker's notes pages to help you deliver an effective, coherent presentation.

The best way to work on your notes is in Notes Page view, shown in Figure 23.1. Each notes page is divided into two parts. A small version of the slide appears at the top of the page, and your notes appear below it.

 Larger Notes   The text in the Notes area in Figure 23.1 is 24-point. You can change the font size in the Notes area, just as you change the font anywhere else in PowerPoint, to make your notes easier to read.

The slide part of each notes page comes from the actual slides you have been creating so far in this book. All you need to do now is type the notes.

You can type notes in Normal view, in the Notes pane, or you can type in Notes Page view. To use Notes Page view, follow these steps:

1. Open the presentation for which you want to create speaker's notes pages.

Slide   Zoom control

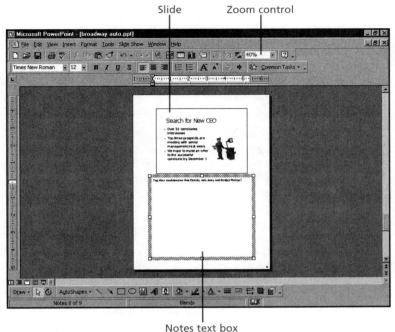

Notes text box

FIGURE 23.1   Example of a speaker's notes page.

2. Choose View, Notes Page to switch to Notes Page view. The currently selected slide appears in Notes Page view, as shown in Figure 23.1.

3. Click the Notes text box in the lower half of the notes page to select it.

4. If desired, change the zoom so you can see what you are typing a little better. Open the Zoom Control drop-down list on the Standard toolbar and click a zoom percentage (refer to Figure 23.1). 100% works well.

5. Type the text that you want to use as notes material for this slide. (You can include reminders, jokes, supporting data, or explanations about how the slide fits in with the presentation's big picture.)

6. Press the Page Up or Page Down key to move to another notes page, and then repeat step 5.

7. Format your text if you want. (For details on how to format text, refer to Lesson 12, "Creating Columns and Lists," and Lesson 13, "Changing the Look of Your Text.")

 Save Your Notes When typing your notes, don't forget to save your work on a regular basis. Once you save and name your presentation file, saving again is as simple as pressing Ctrl+S.

CHANGING THE SIZE OF THE SLIDE AND TEXT BOX

As explained earlier in this lesson, each notes page contains two objects: a slide and a text box. You change the size of either object just as you change the size of any object in PowerPoint (see Lesson 19, "Positioning and Sizing Objects").

1. Click the slide's picture or text box to select it. (If you click the text box, a frame appears around it. Click the frame to display handles.)

2. Move the mouse pointer over one of the object's handles. (Use a corner handle to change both the width and height of the object. Use a side, top, or bottom handle to change only one dimension at a time.)

3. Hold down the mouse button and drag the handle until the object is the size you want.

4. Release the mouse button.

Consistent Notes Pages   To keep the size of the slides and note text boxes consistent on all notes pages, change the size on the Notes Master. The following section explains how to display and work with the Notes Master.

WORKING WITH THE NOTES MASTER

Just as a slide show has a Slide Master that contains the background and layout for all the slides in the presentation, the Notes Master contains the background and layout for all your notes pages. You can use the Notes Master to do the following:

- Add background information (such as the date, time, or page numbers) you want to appear on all the notes pages.

- Add a picture, such as a company logo, that you want to appear on each notes page.

- Move or resize objects on the notes pages.

- Choose a color scheme or background for the slide. (This affects the look of the slide only on the notes pages, not in the presentation itself.)

- Set up the Body Area of the Notes Master to control the general layout and formatting of the text in the notes area of each notes page.

To change the Notes Master, perform the following steps:

1. Select View, Master, Notes Master, or hold down Shift as you click the Notes Pages View button. The Notes Master appears. See Figure 23.2.

2. Change any of the elements in the Notes Master as you would in Slide Master.

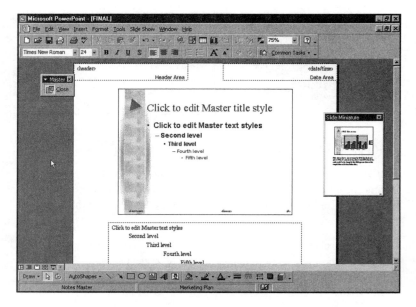

FIGURE 23.2   Edit the Notes Master just as you did the Slide Master in Lesson 8.

In this lesson, you learned how to create speaker's notes pages to help in the delivery of a presentation. In the next lesson, you learn how to create audience handouts.

LESSON 24

CREATING AUDIENCE HANDOUTS

In this lesson, you learn how to create handouts to distribute to your audience.

HOW HANDOUTS HELP YOUR AUDIENCE

Most presenters move through a presentation fairly quickly, giving the audience little time to filter through all the data on the slides. Because of this, it is often useful to give the audience handouts or copies of the presentation slides so they can follow along with you. You do this by printing a replica of your slide show on paper, or by printing several slides per page.

PRINTING HANDOUTS

Creating handouts is fairly easy. Follow these steps:

1. Choose File, Print. The Print dialog box opens.

2. Open the Print What drop-down list, and choose Handouts.

3. In the Handouts area, open the Slides Per Page drop-down list and choose 2, 3, 4, 6, or 9 slides to print per page. See Figure 24.1.

4. Make any other selections in the Print dialog box, such as Number of Copies. Then click OK to print. (For more details on how to print, refer to Lesson 7, "Printing Presentations, Notes, and Handouts.")

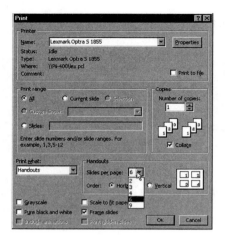

FIGURE 24.1   You can choose the number of slides per page.

 Printing in One Color   If you don't have a color printer, select the Grayscale check box in the Print dialog box. This option formats your output for a one-color printout.

DISPLAYING THE HANDOUT MASTER

The Handout Master controls the placement and look of the slides on the audience handouts. The slide image placeholders on the Handout Master show you where you can place slides on a handout. To display the Handout Master, perform the following steps:

1. Select View, Master, Handout Master or hold down the Shift key and click the Slide Sorter View button. The Handout Master appears, as shown in Figure 24.2.

2. Zoom in so you can see what you're doing. Choose a zoom percentage—66% works well—from the Zoom drop-down list on the Standard toolbar.

Exit the Handout Master   Zoom control

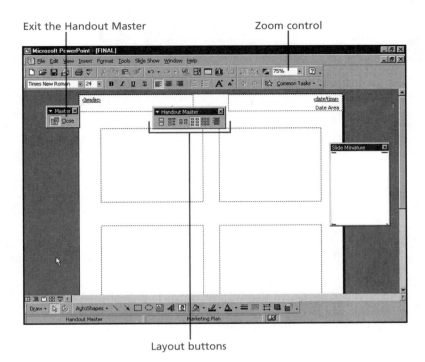

Layout buttons

FIGURE 24.2   The Handout Master.

3. Click one of the Layout buttons to change to the print layout you want to affect. There are separate Handout Master layouts for each number of slides per page.

4. Make any changes to the Handout Master that you want to appear on all handouts. For instance, you might want your company's name and logo, along with today's date, on each page of the handouts.

5. Click the Close button to exit the Handout Master.

6. Print your handouts, as described earlier in this lesson.

In this lesson, you learned how to create audience handouts to accompany your slide presentation. In the next lesson, you learn how to present a slide show onscreen.

LESSON 25

PRESENTING AN ONSCREEN SLIDE SHOW

In this lesson, you learn how to view a slide show onscreen, make basic movements within a presentation, and set show options.

VIEWING AN ONSCREEN SLIDE SHOW

Before you take your presentation "on the road" to show to your intended audience, you should run through it several times on your own computer, checking that all the slides are in the right order and that the timings and transitions between the slides work correctly.

You can preview a slide show at any time to see how the show looks to your audience. To view a slide show, perform the following steps:

1. Open the presentation you want to view.

2. Choose Slide Show, View Show or press F5. The first slide in the presentation appears full-screen.

3. To display the next or previous slide, do one of the following:

    • To display the next slide, click the left mouse button, press the Page Down key, or press the right-arrow or down-arrow key.

    • To display the previous slide, click the right mouse button, press the Page Up key, or click on the left-arrow or up-arrow key.

    • To quit the slide show, press the Esc key.

Start the Show! You can also start a slide show by clicking the Slide Show button in the bottom left corner of the presentation window and by choosing View, Slide Show. However, these ways both start with the currently selected slide, whereas the Slide Show, View Show and F5 methods always start with the first slide.

CONTROLLING THE SLIDE SHOW

While you view a slide show, you can do more than just move from slide to slide. When you move your mouse, notice the triangle in a box at the bottom left corner of the slide show (see Figure 25.1). Click it, or right-click anywhere, for a pop-up menu that contains commands you can use as you actually give the presentation.

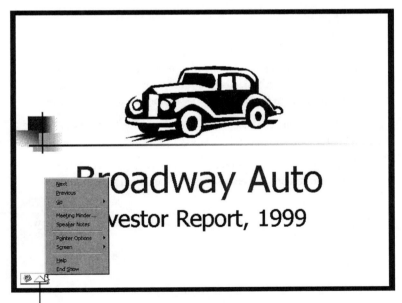

Click here to open the menu, or right-click anywhere.

FIGURE 25.1 You can control the slide show while you present it with this menu.

- The Next and Previous commands enable you to move from slide to slide. (It's easier to change slides using other methods, though.)

- Choose Go, Slide Navigator to bring up a dialog box listing every slide in the presentation. You can jump quickly to any slide with it. You can also jump to a slide with a specific title (if you know it) by selecting Go, Title, and choosing the title from the list.

- Click Meeting Minder to bring up a window where you can take notes as the meeting associated with your presentation progresses.

- Choose Speaker Notes to view your notes for the slide. The audience will see the notes too, unless you are using a two-monitor or monitor-and-projector setup.

- Choose Slide Meter to open a dialog box that enables you to control the timing between slides.

- Arrow and Pen are mouse options. Arrow is the default. Your mouse can serve as an arrow, to point out parts of the slide, or as a pen, to write comments on the slide or circle key areas as you give your presentation. Keep in mind, however, that it is very difficult to write legibly using an ordinary mouse or trackball.

- Pointer Options enables you to choose a color for the pen, and whether to display or hide the pointer.

- Screen opens a submenu that enables you to pause the show, blank the screen, and erase any pen marks you made on the slide.

- End Show takes you back to PowerPoint's slide editing window.

SETTING SLIDE SHOW OPTIONS

Depending on the type of show you're presenting, you may find it useful to make some adjustments to the way the show runs, such as making it run in a window (the default is full-screen) or showing only certain slides. You'll find these controls and more in the Set Up Show dialog box (see Figure 25.2). To open it, choose Slide Show, Set Up Show.

FIGURE 25.2   Use the Set Up Show dialog box to give PowerPoint some basic instructions about how to present your slide show.

In this dialog box, you can do the following:

- Choose what medium the presentation is going to be shown in. Your choices are Presented by a speaker (full-screen), Browsed by an individual (window), and Browsed at a kiosk (full-screen).

- Choose whether to loop the slide show continuously or just show it once. You might want to loop it continuously for it to run unaided at a kiosk at a trade show, for instance.

- Show without narration, if you have created any.

- Show without animation, if you have added any. (You learned about animation in Lesson 22, "Transitions and Animation.")

- Show all the slides or a range of them (which you enter in the From and To boxes).

- Choose a custom show, if you have created one. (To create a custom show—for instance one that contains a subset of the main show's slides—select Slide Show, Custom Show.)

- Choose whether to advance slides manually or use timings you set up. (You learned to add timings in Lesson 22.)

- Choose a pen color. When you are giving a presentation, you can right-click and choose Pointer Options, Pen to turn your mouse pointer into a drawing tool.

In this lesson, you learned how to display a slide presentation onscreen and move between slides, and how to set slide show options. In the next lesson, you learn to create self-running or interactive shows.

LESSON 26

CREATING SELF-RUNNING OR INTERACTIVE SHOWS

In this lesson, you learn how to build controls into a slide show so that the audience can see the show without assistance.

SETTING UP A SELF-RUNNING SHOW

In a self-running show, the slide show runs itself. Each slide advances after a specified period of time, and the audience has no opportunity to control it. This differs from a user-interactive show, discussed later in this lesson, in which the audience can control which slides to see and how quickly to advance.

SETTING SLIDE TIMINGS

For a self-running show, you must set timings. You can set the same timing for all slides (for example, a 20-second delay between each slide), or you can set a separate timing for each slide individually.

First, configure the show to use timings by following these steps:

1. Choose Slide Show, Set Up Show. The Set Up Show dialog box appears. (You dealt with this in Lesson 25, "Presenting an Onscreen Slide Show," so it should be familiar.)

2. Click the Using Timings, If Present option button.

3. Click OK.

Next, set the timings. The default timing for each slide is None, which means the speaker or audience must advance the slides manually, as you learned in Lesson 25. When you set timing for a transition between two slides, you are specifying the amount of time the first slide will appear onscreen before the next slide moves in to take its place.

Follow these steps to set an automatic timing for a slide (or for all slides):

1. Switch to Slide Sorter view (View, Slide Sorter).

2. (Optional) If you want to set the timing for an individual slide, or for a group of slides, select the slides you want to affect.

3. Choose Slide Show, Slide Transition. The Slide Transition dialog box appears.

4. In the Advance area, click to place a check mark in the Automatically After check box.

On Mouse Click   If you are going to provide a mouse for audience use, leave the On Mouse Click check box marked in the Advance section. That way, if the reader finishes reading the slide before the specified delay, he can click to advance the slide show without waiting.

5. Enter an amount of time to wait (see Figure 26.1). For example, to wait 20 seconds, enter 00:20 or click the up arrow button next to the field until 00:20 is displayed there.

FIGURE **26.1**   Enter the delay between this slide and the next one.

6. To apply the change to the selected slide(s), click Apply, or to apply it to all the slides in the presentation, click Apply to All.

REHEARSING TIMINGS

It can be hard to gauge how much time to assign to each slide when you're "out of context." It's much easier to actually display the slide show and keep track of how much time you spend reading each slide.

The Rehearse Timings feature does just that; it enables you to run the slide show and automatically track the time you spend on each slide. Then it applies those times to the slides, just as if you had entered them yourself using the procedure in the preceding section.

To use Rehearse Timings, follow these steps:

1. Choose Slide Show, Rehearse Timings. The slide show starts, with a Rehearsal toolbar onscreen.

2. Advance through the presentation normally (see Lesson 25). The Rehearsal toolbar times you (see Figure 26.2).

3. If you need to pause the show (for example, to answer the phone), click the Pause button. Then click it again to resume when you're ready.

4. When you reach the end of the slide show, a message appears telling you how long it took and asking whether you want to record the new timings. Click Yes. The new timings are assigned to each slide.

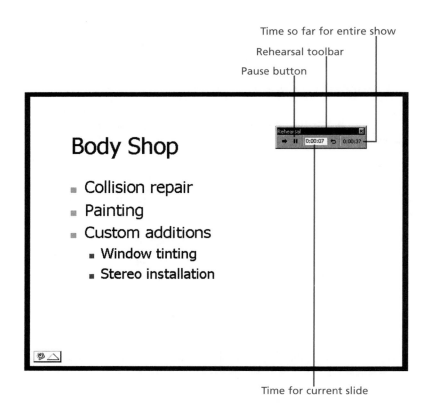

Time so far for entire show

Rehearsal toolbar

Pause button

Body Shop

- Collision repair
- Painting
- Custom additions
  - Window tinting
  - Stereo installation

Time for current slide

FIGURE 26.2   Display the slide show as you run through your narration or read the slides out loud to set the amount of time for each slide to remain onscreen.

CREATING A USER-INTERACTIVE SHOW

In a user-interactive show, you provide the audience some means of controlling the show. You can simply provide access to a keyboard or mouse, and let them control the show in the same way you learned in Lesson 25, or you can provide action buttons onscreen that make it easy for them to jump to specific slides.

SETTING THE SLIDE SHOW FOR MANUAL ADVANCE

Earlier in this lesson, you saw how the Set Up Show dialog box enables you to choose between automatic and manual advance. For a user-interactive presentation, you will want to have the slides advance manually, since different people read at different speeds. Revisit this dialog box (Slide Show, Set Up Show) and make sure that Manually is chosen in the Advance Slides area.

ADDING ACTION BUTTONS ON SLIDES

As you saw in Lesson 25, one way to advance or go back in a slide show is to press the Page Down key or Page Up key on the keyboard. This simple method works fine, except for two things:

- In a kiosk-type setting, in which a self-running show runs continuously without supervision, you may not want the audience to have access to the computer's keyboard.

- This method simply plods from slide to slide, with no opportunity to jump to special slides or jump to the beginning or end quickly.

A better way is to add *action buttons* to your slides. Action buttons are like controls on an audio CD player—they let you jump to any slide quickly, go back, go forward, or even stop the presentation.

 Same Controls on All Slides? If you want to add the same action buttons to all slides in the presentation, add the action buttons to the Slide Master. To display the Slide Master, select View, Master, Slide Master.

To add an action button to a slide, follow these steps:

1. Display the slide in Normal or Slide view.

2. Select Slide Show, Action Buttons, and pick a button from the palette that appears next to the command (see Figure 26.3). For instance, if you want to create a button that advances to the next slide, you might choose the button with the arrow pointing to the right.

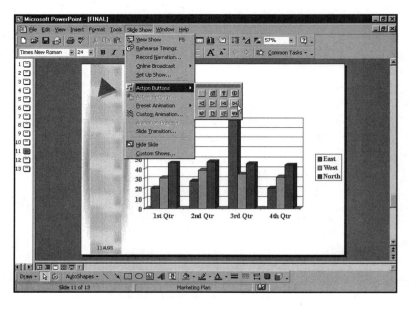

FIGURE 26.3 Choose the button that you think your reader will most strongly identify with the action you're going to assign to it.

Which Button Should I Choose? Choose any button you like; at this point you are only choosing a picture to show on the button, not any particular function for it. However, you might consider the action that you want the button to perform, and then pick a button picture that matches it well. To change the button picture, you must delete the button and create a new one.

3. Your mouse pointer turns into a crosshair. Drag to draw a box on the slide where you want the button to appear. (You can resize it later if you want, the same way you resized graphics in Lesson 19, "Positioning and Sizing Objects.") PowerPoint draws the button on the slide and opens the Action Settings dialog box (see Figure 26.4).

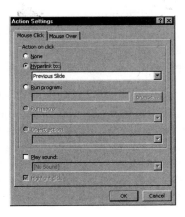

FIGURE 26.4 You can control the way one slide transitions to the next with the Action Settings dialog box.

4. Choose the type of action you want to happen when the user clicks the button. Most of the time you will choose Hyperlink To, but your complete list of choices is

- **None**

- **Hyperlink to** This can be a slide, an Internet hyperlink, a document on your computer—just about anything.

- **Run Program** You can choose to have a program start when the user clicks on the button.

- **Run Macro** If you have recorded a macro, you can have the user run it from the button.

- **Object Action** If you have embedded (OLE) objects in the presentation, you can activate one when the button is clicked.

5. Open the drop-down list for the type of action you chose, and select the exact action (for instance, Next Slide). Or, if you chose Run Program, click the Browse button and locate the program to be run.

6. (Optional) If you want a sound to play when the user clicks the button, select the Play Sound check box and choose a sound from the drop-down list.

7. (Optional) If you want it to look highlighted when the user clicks the button (a nice little extra), leave the Highlight Click check box marked.

8. Click OK. Your button appears on the slide.

9. View the presentation (as you learned at the beginning of Lesson 25) to try out the button.

Figure 26.5 shows three buttons added to a slide. Actually, they were added to the Slide Master, so the same buttons appear on each slide in the presentation. This kind of consistency gives the reader a feeling of comfort and control.

 No Controls on Slide 1 When you add action buttons to the Slide Master, they appear on every slide except the first one in the presentation. If you want action buttons on the first slide, you must add them specifically to that slide or to the Title Master.

 Don't Group Each action button must be an independent object on the slide. Don't group them together or they won't work properly.

 Make Your Own Buttons To create a custom action button with your own text on it, select the blank button and then type in it after you create it.

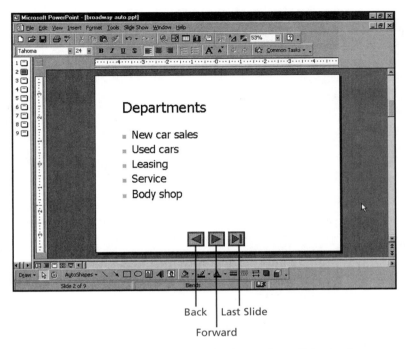

Back | Last Slide
Forward

FIGURE 26.5 These control buttons display various slides in the presentation.

In this lesson, you learned how to set up shows to be self-running or user-interactive. You can then distribute such presentations on disk, set them up to run unaided at trade shows, or even make them available over the Internet. In the next lesson, you learn about some special considerations for creating a show to be delivered over the Internet.

LESSON 27

DESIGNING A PRESENTATION FOR THE INTERNET

In this lesson, you learn how PowerPoint makes it easy to publish your presentations on the World Wide Web or your corporate intranet.

SPECIAL CONSIDERATIONS FOR DESIGNING WEB SHOWS

The World Wide Web is the most popular and graphical component of the Internet, a worldwide network of computers. Many businesses maintain Web sites containing information about their products and services for public reading. Still other businesses maintain an internal version of the Web that's strictly for employee use, and they use the company's local area network to make it available to its staff. These are called *intranets*.

Sooner or later, you may be asked to prepare a PowerPoint presentation for use on a Web site or an intranet. Don't panic! It's simpler than it sounds.

Creating a presentation for Web distribution is much like creating any other user-interactive presentation (see Lesson 26, "Creating Self-Running or Interactive Shows"). However, consider these factors when dealing with the Web:

- For your viewers' convenience, keep the file size as small as possible. That means don't use gratuitous graphics, sounds, or movies.

- You should include action buttons on each slide that enable the user to jump to the previous and next slides, and possibly other action buttons too. See Lesson 26 for information about action buttons.

- If you want the users to be able to jump from your presentation to other Web sites, make sure you include the appropriate hyperlinks. See the following section for details.

- If you convert the presentation to HTML (Web) format, anyone with a Web browser can view it on the Internet, but the presentation may not be exactly the same as the PowerPoint version of it. Depending on the Web browser used to view it, sounds, movies, transitions, and other features may not play correctly.

- If you distribute the file in PowerPoint format, your audience must have PowerPoint installed on their PCs, or must download a special PowerPoint Viewer (discussed later in this lesson).

ADDING URL HYPERLINKS

Remember back in Lesson 26 when we added action buttons to a slide? The action buttons moved us from slide to slide in the presentation. These were hyperlinks. You can also assign links to Web addresses (URLs) to a button. For instance, you might have a button that takes you to your company's home page (the top page at their Internet site) at the bottom of every slide.

A hyperlink can be attached to an action button or to some other graphic, or it can be attached to a string of text characters.

ASSIGNING A HYPERLINK TO AN ACTION BUTTON OR GRAPHIC

The following steps show you how to assign a hyperlink to an action button:

1. Choose Slide Show, Action Buttons, and then choose a button to place on the slide, as you learned in Lesson 26. For example, use the one that looks like a house to hyperlink to your company's home page.

2. When the Action Settings dialog box appears, click the Hyperlink To option button, and then choose URL from the Hyperlink To drop-down list. See Figure 27.1.

FIGURE 27.1   Choose URL from the Hyperlink To list.

3. The Hyperlink to URL dialog box appears.

4. Enter the Web address in the URL text box (see Figure 27.2). Then click OK.

FIGURE 27.2   Enter the URL (the Web address) to which you want to hyperlink.

5. Click OK to close the Action Settings dialog box.

If you have already created an action button, and you want to change its hyperlink, select the button and choose Slide Show, Action Settings. Then pick up the preceding steps at step 2. You can also assign a hyperlink to any graphic in this same way; select the graphic and then choose Slide Show, Action Settings.

CREATING A TEXT-BASED HYPERLINK

You can either insert a "bare" hyperlink, in which the text is the same as the URL, or you can assign a URL to some existing text. Follow these steps:

1. (Optional) To use existing text, select it.

2. Choose Insert, Hyperlink or press Ctrl+K. The Insert Hyperlink dialog box opens.

3. The text you selected in step 1 appears in the Text to Display box. If you want to change it, do so; or if you didn't type any text in step 1, type some now. For example, if the URL will take them to your home page, you might type **Click here to visit our home page**.

4. Click the Existing File or Web Page button.

5. Enter the Web page's URL in the Type the file or Web page name text box (see Figure 27.3).

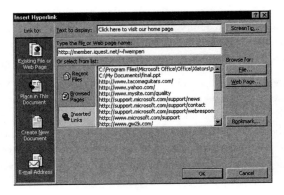

FIGURE 27.3   Enter the Web page address (its URL).

6. Click OK. The selected text appears underlined and in a different color, indicating that it is a hyperlink.

Auto URL Entry If you don't know the Web page's address, click the Web Page button to open your Web browser. Navigate to the page you want to link to, and then jump back to PowerPoint (by clicking the PowerPoint presentation's name on the Windows taskbar). The URL is automatically entered for you.

TESTING THE HYPERLINK

To test your hyperlink, view the slide in Slide Show view, and click the button with your mouse. Your Web browser should start and the selected URL should load in it. If it doesn't work, check to make sure you entered the URL correctly. If it is correct, check your Internet connection, or try again later. (Sometimes a Web page may be temporarily unavailable.)

SAVING A PRESENTATION IN HTML FORMAT

PowerPoint has the capability to save a presentation in HTML format, so it can be viewed using any Web browser. Since all World Wide Web users have Web browser programs, no one need miss out on your presentation.

The quality of the translation has improved considerably in PowerPoint 2000 over previous PowerPoint versions. PowerPoint 2000 saves in a Web format that allows your sounds, movies, animations, and other special effects to be seen just as you intended, provided the person viewing the presentation has a capable Web browser (Internet Explorer 4.0 or higher is best.) With other Web browsers, not all special effects may appear, but at least the basic presentation (the slide text and graphics) will be shown.

To save a presentation in HTML format, follow these steps:

1. Choose File, Save As Web Page. The Save As dialog box appears (see Figure 27.4).

FIGURE 27.4   Choose a name for your saved Web presentation.

2. In the File Name text box, enter a file name for the first page of the presentation (the title slide). By default this is the name of your presentation file.

3. (Optional) If you want the page title (the name in the title bar when the page is displayed in a Web browser) to be different than the one shown, click the Change button and enter a different title.

4. Click Save. Your presentation is saved.

Publishing Options   Users of PowerPoint 97 may be wondering where all the special Web-saving options went that they used to be able to set. They're still there; they're just hidden.

Notice that in the Save As dialog box (Figure 27.4), there is a Publish button. Click it to go to a Publish as Web Page dialog box in which you can set all kinds of options, including which Web browser your audience will likely use and which slides to include.

Within that Publish as Web Page dialog box, there is a Web Options button. Click it to open the Web Options dialog box, where you can choose even more special settings.

A saved HTML presentation is actually many files, not a single one. PowerPoint creates a home page (an entry point) with the same name as the original presentation. (This is the file you were naming when you chose a name in step 2 of the preceding list.) For example, if the presentation file was named Broadway.ppt, the home page would be named Broadway.htm. Then it creates a folder named {presentation name} Files (for example, Broadway Files) that contains all the other HTML, graphics, and other files needed to display the complete presentation. If you are transferring the HTML presentation to another PC (which is very likely, if you are going to make it available on the Internet through your company's server), you must transfer not only the lone HTML home page but also the entire associated folder.

TRANSFERRING YOUR WEB PRESENTATION TO AN INTERNET SERVER

To make your Web presentation available to others on the Internet, you must copy it to your company's Web server or your Internet service provider's server. Find out from your system administrator the full path of the location where you should store your files.

One way to transfer the files is to use an FTP (file transfer protocol) program to upload the files to the appropriate directory on the server. This method is fairly easy, but if you do not have an FTP program, you must find and download one. A good one is WS_FTP, available from http://www.shareware.com.

You may also be able to save the presentation directly to the server through the Save As dialog box (Figure 27.4). In the Save As Web Page dialog box, open the Save In drop-down list and choose Add/Modify FTP Locations; set up the location, and then choose that location to save to. This is a very efficient method, as it saves a few steps over saving and then transferring.

One final way to transfer your work to a Web server is the Web Publishing Wizard that comes with Windows 98. Choose Start, Programs, Internet Explorer, Web Publishing Wizard, and follow the prompts to transfer a single file or a single folder at a time. You will have to run it twice—once for the starting file and once for the accompanying folder.

USING THE POWERPOINT VIEWER

Instead of saving your work as a Web page, you can simply copy the PowerPoint presentation in its native .ppt format to the Web server and let the readers access it as a PowerPoint presentation. This is good because it preserves all your special effects, no matter what browser the audience is using; it does, however, require that all your readers have a copy of PowerPoint installed.

A partial solution for this situation is to provide your audience with a PowerPoint viewer program. This program is a "runtime" version of PowerPoint, containing just enough of the right stuff to view your presentation onscreen. The reader can't make any changes to the presentation; it's like being permanently in Slide Show view.

You can install the PowerPoint Viewer from the PowerPoint (or Office) setup program. Just pop the CD-ROM back in your drive, use Maintenance Mode's Add or Remove Features command to add components, and add the PowerPoint Viewer. (It's under Microsoft PowerPoint for Windows, and it's called PPT Files Viewer.)

The PowerPoint Viewer is free and freely distributed, so you can provide a copy to all your users on your intranet, or you can provide a link to the viewer on your company's Web site so that anyone who doesn't yet have the viewer can download it directly from Microsoft. After users have the PowerPoint viewer, and have downloaded your presentation file from the Web, they can run the viewer like any program and load the presentation file into it to view it. Figure 27.5 shows a presentation being loaded for viewing in the PowerPoint viewer.

FIGURE 27.5   You can't give everyone a copy of PowerPoint, but it's perfectly legal to give everyone the PowerPoint viewer.

 Presentation Broadcasting   You can give a presentation "live" over a network (or the Internet) with the new Presentation Broadcasting feature in PowerPoint 2000. For more information about this, see the PowerPoint 2000 Help system or pick up *Special Edition Using Microsoft PowerPoint 2000*, also published by Macmillan Publishing.

In this lesson, you learned about PowerPoint's capabilities in helping you present your slides on the Web.

Congratulations! You now know the basics of PowerPoint, and you're ready to start creating your own presentations. If you want to learn more, pick up a more advanced PowerPoint book by Macmillan, such as *Special Edition Using Microsoft PowerPoint 2000*, by Patrice Rutledge, or explore the PowerPoint 2000 Help system at your leisure. Good luck, and may all your presentations be successful!

INDEX

B

C